Additional Praise for

A Gift of Age
Old Lesbian Life Stories

The amazing old women revealed in these stories, courageous and inspiring in the varied ways they found their truth and reinvented their lives, form the very roots of who we are and where we are today as a community. These fascinating, colorful oral histories couldn't be more vital to us all — they are the building blocks of our history. To read these stories, this sharing of lives, is to be proud. And grateful.

Katherine Forrest, author of the lesbian classic
Curious Wine and the Kate Delafield mystery series

What a gift it is to contribute stories to the collective memory of this great planet. I hope that when we read someone's story, it inspires us to leave our own story — told to a friend, spoken into a tape recorder, typed on to a computer, sent longhand to a grandchild. When one has lived through the silencing that comes with oppression, fear, and invisibility, it is of utmost importance to make a special effort in leaving the gift of story. Thank you to the Old Lesbian Oral Herstory Project for this gift.

Holly Near, singer, author and teacher

A Gift of Age provides a guarantee that our generation of old lesbians will not slip into oblivion as former generations have been allowed to do. As an old lesbian myself (born January 1932), I find these, my sisters' stories, to be moving, challenging, and encouraging. We are a distinguished group!

Virginia Ramey Mollenkott, Ph.D, English Professor
Emeritus and author of 13 books, including
Sensuous Spirituality: Out from Fundamentalism (2008)

A GIFT OF AGE
OLD LESBIAN LIFE STORIES

A COLLECTION OF STORIES
BASED ON INTERVIEW TRANSCRIPTS
IN THE OLD LESBIAN
ORAL HERSTORY PROJECT

A Gift of Age: Old Lesbian Life Stories
by Arden Eversmeyer and Margaret Purcell

© **Copyright 2009**
ISBN 978-0-9823669-6-7

Second Printing: 2010

Publisher Cataloging in Publication
Eversmeyer, Arden.
    A gift of age. Old lesbian life stories : a collection of stories based on interview transcripts in the Old Lesbian Oral Herstory Project / [by Arden Eversmeyer and Margaret Purcell].
        p. : ill. ; cm.
    Includes index.
    ISBN: 978-0-9823669-6-7
    1. Lesbians--United States--Anecdotes. 2. Lesbians--United States--History. 3. Old Lesbian Oral Herstory Project. 4. Lesbians' writings. I. Purcell, Margaret (Margaret Christine), 1951- II. Title. III. Title: Old lesbian life stories

PS508.L47 E94 2009
810.8/0353

Cost of a single copy within the United States: $16.95
Discounts available for bulk and library orders. Contact us for details.

Contact the Old Lesbian Oral Herstory Project at:

> OLOHP
> PO Box 980422
> Houston, TX 77098
> e-mail: info@olohp.org
> website: www.olohp.org

Dedications

**To the women who shared the stories
used to create this collection.**

**To all the other women who have generously
provided their herstory for the
Old Lesbian Oral Herstory Project.**

Acknowledgments

In addition to all the women who shared their stories, we want to acknowledge Old Lesbians Organizing for Change, the premier organization dedicated to improving the lives of Old Lesbians. OLOC has sponsored the Old Lesbian Oral Herstory Project since 2002.

We would also like to thank Pokey Anderson. Pokey provided a critical eye to this book project as someone who transcribed several of the original interviews. She also wrote the first published magazine article* based on the stories in the OLOHP.

Special thanks go to Deb and Joanne who provided the final push it took to move the creation of this book from our wish list to reality.

In keeping with the "it takes a village" concept, we would be remiss if we didn't extend our heartfelt appreciation to all of the women who generously shared their time and expertise.

We count our blessings daily for our unbelievably supportive and patient partners, Charlotte and Mary.

Rebels & Survivors: The life stories of four of our lesbian ancestors was published in OutSmart Magazine in March 2001. A copy can be accessed at www.outsmartmagazine.com/issue/i03-01/lesbian.html

Contents

⸙

The Stories

Author's Preface

Arden:

I gave an interview more than fifteen years ago to a student. It was about my life as a lesbian, more specifically, as an old lesbian. At that time, I was 60 and I said I thought my life could be neatly divided into three parts. The first part included my childhood, teenage years and coming out to myself in college as I gained an understanding of why I felt I was different. Next, I spent 33 years living in a long-term relationship with Tommie. That part ended when she died and I was given the chance and the challenge to start again. The third part of my life began with a five-year process of taking my power and healing. I also developed my social consciousness and became an activist during this time.

It all seemed nice and neat. I knew my life wasn't over, but I didn't have any great expectations of what was yet to come. And I certainly didn't think I would fall in love again, but I did. And I never expected to find a new direction for my life—collecting the life stories of old lesbians. So, when I wasn't even looking, both my sugar, Charlotte, and this project found me, and I began a fourth part in my life.

Those few years I spent transitioning from the third to the fourth part, I often thought about how old lesbians are, in many ways, an invisible population. It was easy to see how that came about, given how we lived. I had never been out to anyone other than close friends and that was how they lived too. Then a woman I knew died. She had some great tales she loved to tell, and I found it disturbing that her story would only live on with a few friends. And that's when it began.

Something began to nudge me. I kept thinking about all the old lesbians I knew and the stories they had to tell. As scary as it was, the idea that I could be the one to document their stories just wouldn't let me go.

It started out as something simple, me talking with a few friends to make sure their stories were saved. But the project quickly took on a life of its own. Most of the women I talked with connected me with other women they knew, and before I had a chance to think it through, I was traveling all over the country interviewing women.

I'm still not sure I ever had much say in whether or not I wanted to take on such a huge project. Feels more like it took me on. But I do know one thing for sure—I have never regretted it. It's been incredibly rewarding and humbling. I've often said that I fall just a little bit in love with each old lesbian I interview. I'm always honored that they will share their stories with me. I stay in touch with all of them and some have gone on to become good friends. Some have died and that's been hard. Others continue to live such rich lives that I wish I had time to go back and interview them all over again.

There will come a time when I am no longer able to gather stories. Finding lesbians born in the early 1900s will become harder and harder. The Old Lesbian Oral Herstory Project, as I know it, may even come to an end. I'm okay with that. I'm confident the stories in the collection will have done what I want; they've created a first-hand record of the diverse experiences of these women. And maybe someone else will take up the mantle and focus on collecting the stories of lesbians born in the mid 1900s. They have their own unique stories to tell.

Now, there is this book. And a website (www.olohp.org). And we're working on ways to share more of the collection. It makes my head spin. And at the same time, it pleases me no end to see these stories being shared—shared with other old lesbians, with younger lesbians, and with society at large.

The stories deserve to be told. I am truly humbled by the thought that I actually played a pivotal role in making this happen.

What a ride! And, best of all, it's not over.

Arden Eversmeyer

Margaret:

The longer I live, the more conflicted I am about destiny. I've never believed that individual events are meant to happen, that the details of our daily lives have been laid out in a huge planning book. But when something happens to me, like meeting Arden Eversmeyer, I do have to wonder.

My partner, Mary, became involved with Old Lesbians Organizing for Change, a non-profit that works to improve the lives of old lesbians. Even though I wasn't officially old enough, (you have to be 60 to belong to OLOC), I began tagging along when Mary went to meetings. That's where I met Arden and became aware of her collection of interviews.

There had already been tentative plans to put together a book based on what had become known as the Old Lesbian Oral Herstory Project. A woman had already expressed an interest in writing the book, and preliminary work was underway.

Mary and I traveled to Texas several times over the next few years, getting to know Arden and her sweetie, Charlotte, and learning more and more about the OLOHP. Fascinated by the Project, and looking for a way we could help, Mary and I took on the task of creating an electronic backup copy of all the work Arden had done. It was a time-consuming task that required two additional visits to scan the printed copies of all of the interviews and all of the supporting materials.

Two years later, I heard that the woman who had done the preliminary work for a book based on these stories could not continue, and I e-mailed Arden. Since my writing experience was limited to magazine articles, training materials, newsletters and similar materials, I wasn't sure that my skills were what Arden and the book project needed. In what I characterized as "a really little voice," I broached the possibility of my giving the book a try. I didn't want her to feel obligated by our growing friendship. I was thrilled when I opened my e-mail the next day to find a reply from Arden that started, "Good morning tiny voice."

I had ready access to most of the Herstories, since we had scanned them, and I found myself reading one after another, being pulled into each woman's story. My office was soon over-run with printed transcripts, notes and lists. I love to read in bed, and it became a family joke that I'd go to bed with a different woman each night as I read and reread their interviews. I was soon conferring with Arden about the myriad of details and drafts it has taken to make a book happen.

Sometimes I find myself looking back and shaking my head. Could all of the little events that had to happen precisely when they did to get me here have been just luck? If it was, I'll have to say I'm one of the luckiest people alive.

Margaret Purcell

A note about the graphics in *A Gift of Age*:

Is a picture really worth a thousand words? We think so, and we hope you'll agree. The pictures we had access to for use in this book were all photocopies, and some of them were actually copies of copies! The age and condition of many of the documents were additional limiting factors. Thus, making sure we had adequate quality in this book became quite a task.

We hope you'll agree that though the quality of some of the graphics we've included may leave something to be desired, even the fuzziest among them add to the story, and often tell their own tales.

Introduction

Stories in the Old Lesbian Oral Herstory Project provide a valuable glimpse into what it was like to be a lesbian during a unique period in American history. As more and more people have become aware of this collection of stories, a question has frequently been posed: How can we read them?

For years the sole focus of the OLOHP had been to collect and preserve the stories, with hopes that they would eventually end up in an archive somewhere, adding to historical records about lesbians who were born early in the 1900s. Determining a way to share these stories with a broad audience presented several very interesting obstacles.

The Herstories themselves are printed transcripts that range in length from 10 to 100+ pages. They were not edited by anyone other than the woman who shared her story; some, not even then. So it was not practical to use them in their original format. There are more than 100 completed Herstories, and another 50 or so in various stages of the process. Each woman tells her own story in her own unique voice and style.

Thus, a decision was made to write a book. After several false starts, we realized we needed a clear vision of what the book would be, and an equally clear vision of what the book would not be.

What the book is:

A Gift of Age: Old Lesbian Life Stories is a retelling of the stories of 22 lesbians born in the early part of the 1900s. All of the information in the stories comes from the transcribed interviews; therefore, the stories rely heavily on direct quotes. Women in this book, who were still living when it was being written, were sent a draft of their story and encouraged to make any edits they felt were needed. We strove to ensure that each story conveyed enough information from the original interviews that readers would feel they had met the women, and that the stories shared some details about what it was like to be a lesbian during their lifetime.

In crafting each story, we tried to include insights into what it was like to grow up at a time when a woman had probably never even heard the word "lesbian." There were no books to help her understand what she was going through. There weren't many places to safely go and meet other lesbians. Women had to be careful what they wore to a bar because a woman could be arrested for wearing "men's clothes" such as slacks. This was a time when being out in the workplace was almost unheard of, there were no lesbian organizations, and a woman ran the risk of being hospitalized for treatment simply for loving another woman.

What the book is not:

A Gift of Age does not focus exclusively on lesbian aspects of the women's lives. When a woman was interviewed, she was encouraged to tell her life story, to share whatever she felt was important about her life. The stories in this book tell about their lives, not just their lesbian lives.

The stories in *A Gift of Age*, and in the OLOHP as a whole, may not be a representative sample of lesbians living during this specific time frame. Only those who knew about the Project had a chance to be included. Of those, there were many women who did not feel safe enough with their family and friends to participate. And there were those who, sadly, felt they didn't have a story worth telling. So this book, and the OLOHP collection, is filled with stories from a self-selected group of women who, for us, happened to be at the right place at the right time.

Arden Eversmeyer, the Director of the OLOHP, was the one person familiar enough with each and every story to write a book about them. But she was quick to clarify that her passion lay in collecting the stories, not writing. In her mid-70s herself, Arden felt the Project was best served if she continued to focus on interviewing more old lesbians.

Everyone lucky enough to know Arden understands how much she loves this project and how protective she is of the women who have generously shared their stories. To that end, Arden shared the bulk of the initial writing with Margaret, and stayed integrally involved with the development of the book from beginning to end.

The single hardest step was deciding which stories to include. We wanted a representative sampling from the collection as a whole, but what did that really mean? Did it mean both women who knew they were lesbians all their lives, and women who came to that realization late in life? What about women who knew they were lesbians when they were young, but married anyway because they felt they had no other option? How about women who were only out to a close circle of friends, but never to family or co-workers? When we tried to factor in cultural and socio-economic backgrounds, professions, military experience, ethnicity and religious upbringing, choices became even more difficult.

After almost every conversation about which stories we needed to include, it seemed that the list was longer than when we'd started! That is when it became apparent to us that *A Gift of Age: Old Lesbian Life Stories* was only a beginning. It includes what we hope is a representative sample of the breadth of stories in the collection. Work is already underway for a second and third installment. We plan to focus on stories from couples, both of whom gave interviews, and then shift to stories of early and late bloomers.

It is our hope that after reading this book, you will feel that you know each woman, and that you will have a greater understanding of each woman's circumstances and choices.

When a woman tells the truth, she is creating
the possibility of more truth around her.
Adrienne Rich

The history of all times, and of today especially, teaches that ... women will be forgotten if they forget to think about themselves.

The quote above is from Louise Otto, a German writer, feminist, poet, journalist, and women's rights movement activist. She died in 1895 and, adding weight to her own point, sometimes had to resort to writing under a male pseudonym to be heard.

During Their Lives: A Timeline

We live in such different times now that it can be hard to fully comprehend the forces that influenced the lives of the women in this book.

What might your life have been like if you were a young lesbian in the 1940s or 1950s, before the first lesbian organization of any kind was formed? The President of the United States authorized the firing of any federal employee deemed to be a sexual pervert. Every state considered sex between two women illegal. Lesbians were considered by the medical profession to have a sociopathic personality disturbance that required psychiatric treatment.

Even for people who grew up in more recent, seemingly more accepting times, seeing California issue marriage licenses to same-sex couples, then annul them—not once, but twice—has to give even the most trusting person pause. Imagine how that see-sawing of public opinion probably feels to women who have had to live much of their lives with a justified level of fear and caution.

Thinking about the age these women were when various historical events occurred adds a deeper level of understanding to the unique situations they faced.

	Historical Event
1920s	1920 The 19th Amendment, granting women the right to vote, passes. 1920 The term "gay" is first used in publications. 1929 *The Well of Loneliness* is published in England, and copies are widely destroyed.
1930s	1934 The Hays Code is adopted in Hollywood, banning all references to homosexuality. 1935 Electroshock therapy is declared a successful treatment for homosexuality by the American Psychiatric Association (APA).

Historical Event

<table>
<tr><td>1940s</td><td>1940 Thousands of homosexuals were targeted in the Holocaust.
1942 The US military establishes women's services in the Army, Navy, Coast Guard and Marines.
1943 The US military bans gays and lesbians from serving.
1947 *Vice Versa*, a periodical publication for lesbians, first appears in print.</td></tr>
<tr><td>1950s</td><td>1950 The US Senate condones firing all government employees who are considered "moral perverts."
1952 The APA includes homosexuality as a mental disorder: sociopathic personality disturbance.
1952 Congress bars immigration of gay and lesbian people to the United States.
1953 Eisenhower authorizes the firing of federal employees for sexual perversion.
1953 Government employees on the state, federal and local levels are forced to take a "loyalty oath" that includes swearing they are not homosexual.
1955 The first lesbian organization in the United States, the Daughters of Bilitis, is formed by Del Martin and Phyllis Lyon.
1956 The first national lesbian publication, *The Ladder*, is started. Published by the Daughters of Bilitis, it ran from 1956 to 1970.
1957 Ann Bannon wrote the lesbian pulp fiction book, *Odd Girls Out*. It went on to be one of the best selling paperbacks (of all genres) for that year.
1957 The American Civil Liberties Union (ACLU) issues a statement in support of laws against sodomy and the firing of federal employees based on their homosexuality.
1958 The Supreme Court rules that it is legal to distribute the gay periodical, *Gay*, through the U.S. mail.</td></tr>
</table>

Historical Event

1960s

1960 The Daughters of Bilitis holds a convention, making it the first public gathering of lesbians in the US.

1960 The FDA approves birth control pills.

1961 Illinois becomes the first state to legalize consensual same sex acts.

1963 The Equal Pay Act passes.

1966 The word "lesbian" is used in a Hollywood movie (*The Group*) for the first time.

1966 National Organization for Women (NOW), is formed.

1966 The first gay community center in the US opens.

1968 Homosexuality is changed from sociopathic to sexual deviation by the APA.

1969 Betty Friedan warns members of NOW about the "Lavender Menace," lesbians within its ranks.

1969 The Stonewall riots occur in New York.

1970s

1970 The first Gay Pride Parade/Pride March is held in New York City.

1970 The Vatican reaffirms its edict that homosexuality is a moral aberration.

1972 East Lansing, MI, is the first US city to ban anti-gay practices in hiring.

1972 *MS Magazine* starts publication.

1973 The American Psychiatric Association declares that homosexuality is no longer a mental disorder.

1973 The Lesbian Herstory Archive is formed.

1975 The "loyalty oath" is thrown out, and gays and lesbians are no longer banned from civil service.

1976 The first open lesbian wins custody of her children.

1977 A survey of doctors in Oregon reveals 80% would refuse to treat anyone known to be homosexual.

1977 The National Center for Lesbian Rights forms.

1977 The Astraea Lesbian Foundation for Justice forms.

1978 Openly gay city official, Harvey Milk, is assassinated at the height of Anita Bryant's anti-gay campaign.

1979 100,000 people march on Washington for gay rights.

Historical Event

<table>
<tr><td rowspan="1">1980s</td><td>

1982 Parents, Families & Friends of Lesbians and Gays (PFLAG) forms.

1982 The Equal Rights Amendment fails.

1982 Wisconsin is first to pass a statewide gay rights law.

1982 AIDS is declared the "Gay Plague."

1984 The FBI releases thousands of pages of information it has gathered on gay organizations.

1984 Martina Navratilova openly sits with her lover at Wimbledon.

1986 The Supreme Court upholds Georgia sodomy laws making it one of 24 states where you can be arrested for consensual same-sex acts in your own home.

1987 The 2nd March on Washington for LGBT rights draws 500,000 people making it the largest civil rights demonstration in history to date.

1987 The US Census Bureau states women in American earn 68¢ for every man's dollar.

1987 A conference exclusively for old (60 years plus) lesbians is held in California.

1989 Old Lesbians Organizing for Change (OLOC) forms.

</td></tr>
<tr><td>1990s</td><td>

1990 The US Census includes questions that recognize gay and lesbian couples.

1991 After an 8 year battle, Karen Thompson is granted legal guardianship of her severely injured partner, Sharon, whose family tried to deny Karen any rights.

1991 The National Lesbian Conference is held in Atlanta.

1992 The World Health Organization takes homosexuality off its list of illnesses.

1993 The GLBT March on Washington draws more than a million people.

1993 As ordered by President Clinton, the US military initiates the Don't Ask, Don't Tell policy. The policy bars openly gay individuals from serving but limits the military's actions toward identifying LGBT people who are already serving.

</td></tr>
</table>

Historical Event

<table>
<tr><td>more 1990s</td><td>

1994 The American Medical Association (AMA) goes on record opposing attempts to "cure" homosexuality.

1996 The Defense of Marriage Act (DOMA), banning federal recognition of same-sex marriages, is passed.

1998 Tammy Baldwin becomes the first open lesbian elected to a federal office.

</td></tr>
<tr><td>2000s</td><td>

2000 Civil Unions for same-sex couples are legalized in Vermont.

2003 It is ruled unconstitutional to deny same-sex couples the right to marry in Massachusetts.

2004 Robin Tyler, born 1942, and Diane Olson, born 1953, apply for, and are denied, a marriage license in Beverly Hills, California. They then file suit against the state. (The lawsuit is heard by the California Supreme Court in 2008.)

2004 In February, Del Martin, born 1921, and Phyllis Lyon, born 1924, are issued a license in San Francisco, and are the first same-sex couple to wed there.

2004 In November, marriage licenses issued to same-sex couples in San Francisco are voided by the state.

2005 Canada rules same-sex marriage legal nationwide.

2006 New Jersey grants same-sex couples married in a civil union the same rights as heterosexual couples.

2008 Connecticut legalizes gay marriage.

2008 In May, the California State Supreme Court states same-sex marriages cannot legally be denied in CA.

2008 In June, in recognition of the integral role they played in challenging the prevailing law, Robin Tyler and Diane Olson are issued the first same-sex marriage license, and become the first same-sex couple to legally wed in Los Angeles.

2008 In June, Phyllis Lyon and Del Martin legally wed in San Francisco, CA. They had been together more than 50 years. Two months later, Del died.

</td></tr>
</table>

Historical Event

<table>
<tr><td rowspan="3">more 2000s</td><td>2008</td><td>In November, Proposition 8 passes, revoking the right of same-sex couples to wed in California.</td></tr>
<tr><td>2009</td><td>Same-sex marriage becomes legal in Iowa, Vermont, Maine and New Hampshire. Oregon and Washington pass "everything but marriage" legislation.</td></tr>
<tr><td>2009</td><td>The California Supreme Court upholds Proposition 8, but allows any marriages already performed to stand.</td></tr>
</table>

The Stories

LeClair Bissell

Born May 1928 in Virginia
Interviewed in 2004 at age 76

There are probably people on this island that think Nancy and I used to be lesbians!

Instead of entering a world full of possibilities, LeClair's beginning was untimely, to say the least. Her father had been an ace pilot in World War I, serving as a military aide to General William Mitchell, the man who predicted the attack on Pearl Harbor. Her mother served as General Mitchell's private secretary. She loved her work.

My parents were both in their thirties [when they had me]. They had not expected a child, and they didn't particularly want one. If they were to have one, it was not supposed to be me. It was supposed to be a boy, whom they were going to name Clayton, and he would, of course, go to West Point.

One of the greatest bits of luck in my life was that I was born at a time when women couldn't go to West Point, so I escaped that. That would not have been a success.

Her family moved constantly with her father's military career. A young LeClair avoided making friends, and credits her sense of stability to an aunt who lived with them. By the time she got to college, she calculated that it was the 23rd school she had attended. LeClair spent the last three years of high school at a girls' boarding school.

You may not know that I have been "finished," but I have. That was one of those places where you did not leave the campus without another girl. You each wore your hat. You were inspected to make sure you had gloves, and that your stocking seams were straight.

After finishing her first year in college at age 17, LeClair took advantage of the opportunity to spend three years in Europe, where her father was stationed. When she returned to the States, she entered Randolph-Macon Women's College in Lynchburg, Virginia. "It was right around the corner from where Jerry Falwell now holds court. Endless bad news, it was conservative Christian.... You did not think for yourself; you got squelched."

She was unhappy with both the atmosphere and the academics, so LeClair tried joining a sorority, thinking that might improve the situation.

Wrong! I disapproved of them and I felt I was compromising myself.... After three years in Europe, the idea of going back to that school would be like trying to get gas back into the canister again once it had been set free into the air, and there was no way I was going to do that.

LeClair transferred to a school where her sorority didn't have a chapter. She wanted to put a significant amount of distance between herself and her parents, so she went to the University of Colorado at Boulder. There LeClair finished her baccalaureate degree but developed a drinking problem. "I'd had a not-so-hot experience with a man ... and I thought that my problem was that he had broken my heart."

Leaving Colorado behind her, she made several stops and took several big steps. One of those was moving to California where she became involved with a woman.

She was married and had a couple of kids, and as far as she was concerned she just knew we were in love. She was going to leave her husband. We were going to go off with these two kids. I was horrified. ... So I fled, and told myself that that was only because I had been drinking.

It was easy to excuse her physical involvement with women: it was their idea; there was nothing better to do; or it was a cold night. LeClair recalls sitting on the edge of her bed asking herself, "I wonder if I'm a lesbian?" Suddenly everything made sense, and she watched as her "whole life reassembled itself." Everything fell into place.

That would explain all the guys I had chosen. [Several were questioning whether or not they were gay themselves.] And why I was pleased that they didn't make passes at me. I liked men. I just didn't want to go to bed with them. And if I got kissed by a man, it was not unpleasant, it was a total bore. ... Which was totally different from my one experience in high school, when I'd fallen in love with another girl. I had loved necking with her, even though we had said it was because it was wartime and there weren't any men around.

LeClair's next career step was teaching "bone-head English to engineering students" in Connecticut. Her father, whom she described as a man of his word, let her know in a "ferocious letter" that she had one more year [of his support] during which she could study anything she wanted, but it had better be something that would help her make a living.

"I knew I was in trouble, and I sat down with my friend and we got a whole bunch of lab alcohol ... mixed it up with grapefruit juice, and quietly got drunk." Discussing what she should do, someone suggested, since she liked books, she should become a librarian. Off she went to New York, where she studied and began her work in that field.

Drinking had become a regular part of LeClair's life when she'd been in Europe. "I was able to drink freely, I found that people liked me a lot better when I'd had a few drinks. ... It just simply freed me up. It made me feel normal." For the first few years, getting sick from drinking or suffering from hangovers wasn't a problem, and LeClair was the proverbial life-of-the-party.

The hangovers begin, the interference with function begins, the personality changes begin, and I did get ugly. And I did start making social mistakes. More to the point, since alcohol was becoming increasingly important to me, I couldn't be with any friends who couldn't drink. What would I do with them? So, alcohol chose my friends for me, although I didn't realize it.

Pretty soon I could say to you, when you scolded me, which people were beginning to do, that I didn't drink any more than most of my friends. And it would be true. It just didn't dawn on me that I had selected them for that purpose.

LeClair slid into depression, attempted suicide, and tried to convince herself that she was "just a mental case. ... Nobody had told me that alcohol causes depression. I thought I was depressed, and that was why I was drinking. I knew I was crazy." When she finally realized drinking was the cause of her depression, not the result, LeClair got sober through AA. "I went kicking and screaming. I was lucky."

Sober and working as a librarian, LeClair began taking night courses in psychology. She wanted to be a doctor, but being lesbian, alcoholic, older and female, she didn't think she could do the work.

Then I met a woman who changed my life. She was short, she was stocky, she was arrogant, she was horrid; I didn't like her in any way, and she had been accepted to medical school. And I thought, "If that little bitch can get in, well then I bet I can." I'm still grateful to her.

At age 25, and three years sober [in 1959], LeClair started medical school at Columbia University. "I had to study pretty much as hard as I could to stay in the middle of the class. I had ideas when I went there. I was going to ... be an A student and save the world."

LeClair struggled through medical school and went on to an internship and residency at Roosevelt Hospital in New York. There, she struck a bargain with an administrator. She would work for two years in his field, endocrinology, and, in return, she would then

LeClair at work, 38 years of age.

be free to start an alcoholism and drug program there. Luckily, he kept the bargain, and with funding that LeClair had acquired, she began her work with alcoholism and drug addiction.

Then LeClair met Nancy. They began living together, first as roommates to share expenses. Later, they became lovers.

LeClair had a deep commitment to working with the National Institute of Alcoholism and Alcohol Abuse during the Carter administration. Serving on their Advisory Commission, she faced a dilemma: LeClair felt strongly that a study the Institute was funding was improper.

The young Dr. Bissell challenged the commission, knowing she was probably giving up her chance to work in Washington, DC. In a speech at the council meeting, she asserted it was "totally unethical to let pregnant women continue to drink while you check on the amount of fetal alcohol syndrome their children developed." Faced with LeClair's courage, and her outrage that they would do this without warning the women, the organization was forced to rewrite the grant.

She started working at a treatment center in Rhode Island. LeClair needed to get a job that would make a little money, since she had been working for a pittance. That new job didn't last long. LeClair admits she lacked a for-profit mentality. She objected when, motivated by insurance money, the treatment center wanted to admit people whether or not they really needed to be kept for long periods.

LeClair began to feel ill at this time, but her doctor wouldn't take her concerns seriously. He explained away her symptoms by pointing out she had just moved, had lost her support system and "had every right to be a little depressed." She diagnosed her own symptoms as Cushing's Syndrome, a disorder of the adrenal cortex caused by a tumor in the pituitary gland. Her physician, however, discounted her assessment. In his opinion, LeClair only thought she had Cushing's because she had spent two years studying endocrinology.

Pushing her health issues aside, LeClair took this time between jobs to write, something she'd talked about for years. Publishing gave her name recognition and speaking dates. LeClair's five books focused on treatment for alcoholism among professional communities, starting with doctors and going on to lawyers and nurses. Her studies later included social workers, pharmacists, dentists and professional women who did not work in health care. She also taught summer classes at the University of Utah and Rutgers University in New Jersey.

Nancy and LeClair had decided to leave New York and live part-time at the home they owned on Sanibel Island, Florida. They hadn't been there long when LeClair began to notice scratches that wouldn't heal, and unexplained bruising. After venting with some four-letter words, LeClair marched into her doctor's office and said, "Look at this. I've got Cushing's Syndrome. Now are you going to test me for it, or am I going out to Mayo [Clinic] and sign in as Mary Smith, girl secretary, and pay in traveler's checks?"

Tests were conducted, and her initial diagnosis was confirmed. Damage had been done, however, and it took several years for LeClair to feel better.

In the mid 90s, she lost her keen interest in keeping up with her field, and opted to give up her teaching posts and voluntarily surrendered her medical license.

In retirement, LeClair received numerous recognitions, including the prestigious Elizabeth Blackwell Award from the American Medical Women's Association.

Nancy and LeClair became an important part of Sanibel Island history. They turned over the hundred-year old cottage they'd been sharing to the local Historical Preservation Committee. The notable building was moved, via barge, to its new location in a historic village, and they had a new house built on the same property.

Nancy and LeClair in the Galapogos in 1970

Looking back, LeClair recalls deciding she could help herself out by letting Nancy live with her and care for her dog, allowing her to concentrated on her med-school studies. This would help Nancy out at the same time, since she needed a temporary place to stay while she hunted for an apartment. A temporary visit? "Well, since 1955 ..." That was more than 45 years ago.

> *I think one way we managed to do it is that we started right at the beginning with a lot of space in the relationship. You know, she had her own life and so did I. ... There was never the expectation that I was responsible for making her happy and vice versa.*

Unable to be open during their professional lives, she and Nancy are now both out lesbians on Sanibel Island. In many ways, it couldn't be avoided.

> *Small-town Sanibel was quite aware that these two older women lived together in a house where there was no evidence of husbands or progeny of any kind, just a lot of dogs. I think they knew for quite a while, but I started making it clear. People give the flowers for a church service in honor of something. … Nancy and I did flowers in honor of our fortieth [anniversary]… Some of the congregation came up at coffee hour and congratulated us.*

LeClair feels that, as a regular part of the community since 1983, they have served as a visual record of a long-term lesbian relationship. She also acknowledges that, because of their age, "there are probably people on the island who think Nancy and I used to be lesbians."

LeClair was recently approached to sit on the board of Planned Parenthood of Florida. Abortion rights was a cause of significant importance to LeClair. "I ran an emergency room for a while in New York, to make some money. When I was doing that, I did night and weekend duty. … This was before Roe v. Wade. I presided over the deaths of three women in one night."

She had supported Planned Parenthood for years, but thought this was about money. LeClair let them know that, even if they put her on the board, she wasn't going to increase her donation. "Why do you want me?" she asked. Their answer was, "We need another doctor to decorate the stationery. We need more people from Lee County. And we would like a lesbian to be on the board." She accepted the position, and marveled; this was a first for her — to be selected specifically because she was a lesbian.

Nancy in 1988

With more free time available, LeClair became involved with animals. She formed Chihuahuas Rescue and Transport (rescuing chihuahuas), and began working with CROW (Care and Rehabilitation of Wildlife). They have a clinic on Sanibel that handles nothing but native wildlife.

For years, it was a common site to see LeClair and Nancy canoeing through the mangroves, removing monofilament and other tackle left by fishermen when their lines became tangled in the trees and roots. (Monofilament fishing line is a common cause of injuries and death for wild animals.)

LeClair and Nancy also served on the Executive Committee of the Sanibel Democratic Club. But, as LeClair so concisely stated: "There is a limit to how much you can take of whiney old men veterans. I've done my duty, and got out."

The past few years of her life have brought a new difficulty, as Nancy's health began to fail. "She is an old ninety, and very fragile, and we are going through all the indignities of being very old."

Nancy keeps turning to me thinking I can answer her medical questions, make a miracle, and I can't. ... She's still good company, though we're having more fights. ... It's odd, because one has to learn to fight in a totally different way. The classic fight is: "Where are you going? Why didn't you tell me you were going to do that?" "I did." "No, you didn't." "Nancy, it's been on the calendar for three weeks." "Well, your handwriting is bad."

You know, it's got a funny feel to it, because we have had some rules with living together. Two of them are: we would never lie to each other, and we would not ask each other questions if we weren't prepared to deal with the answer. ... It feels manipulative to have to quarrel in a different way, and to dodge discussion where for years we have been able to work things out. There's no working things out with memory that isn't there anymore. ... It's a peacemaking thing.

LeClair died in 2008. Nancy, her partner of 52 years, died in 2007. Interviewer: Arden Eversmeyer

Ethyl 'Ricci Cortez' Bronson

Born November 1924
in New York
Interviewed in 2008 at age 84

Why not? I've nothing to lose.

Each of us is molded by childhood to some extent. This was especially true for Ethyl. By the time she was high school age the years had already shaped her into a strongly independent young woman. Her career path would quickly take her from an ordinary beginning, working in a factory that made the little sugar roses used to decorate birthday cakes, to a remarkable and lengthy career as an exotic dancer.

Ethyl and her brother had been placed in an orphanage by their birth parents early in their childhoods. They had several placements as foster children and felt lucky that they were always able to stay together. That was the good part. But there was also a dark side to the story.

We did the dishes. We put down the carpeting. We hung the drapes. We dusted. We cleaned. We really didn't have much of a childhood. We were like the caretakers of the house. When we got home from school, we did not go out and play. We had chores to do. They did not include going outside. We did our homework. We did our chores. Had dinner. Did the dishes and went to bed. That was our daily routine.

It wasn't a very happy time in Ethyl's life but she was grateful to be warm, housed and fed. And she feels that she and her brother were treated with respect. The family they lived with were Jewish, as was Ethyl. Although they didn't attend Temple regularly, the home was kosher and they did observe the Jewish holidays.

Ethyl had had enough by the time she was 16. She quit school and went to work in the nearby sugar factory. When the factory had to close down because, during the war, sugar was rationed, she took a series of little jobs.

I was a waitress, and then when I was 18, I went to work in a bar as a cocktail waitress. All this was in New York. I worked as a cocktail waitress, making a lot more money than I had made before, because with cocktails they tip more than when they eat.

I worked in this one bar…Well, it was a strip joint. I didn't know that when I went to work for them. The first night that I was there, I was watching the entertainment and these strippers came around. I would never do such a thing! Famous last words.

Ethyl's birth father came back into her life while she was working in the bar in New York.

He had remarried… and brought me to Chicago where he was living with his new wife, who was ten years older than me [Ethyl was still 18]. … I went to live with him and my stepmother. For the first time in my life I thought I had a real family. Well, she treated me like the maid! Needless to say, we did not get along. I was living with my dad in my home. Why should I be treated like a maid? Scrub floors and all that kind of stuff.

I lived there for two years. I was working all the time I was living with them. She started treating me like the maid. I said,

"This is not going to work." One day, here I am in my dad's house, on my hands and knees, scrubbing the kitchen floor. Deja vu. She comes up behind me and says to me, "You missed a spot." Now, I'm eighteen; she's twenty-eight. I stood up and I said, "If you don't like the way I'm doing it, do it yourself." And we got into a hell of a fist-fight. We really did. She had no right to treat me like that!

Ethyl's father hadn't known how she was being treated and was torn between his wife and his daughter.

I did not ask him to choose between us. I left the house ... it was probably about 1946 ... I left the house about midnight, I think, in February. Cold. I just had on a coat and high-heeled shoes, no stockings. I was hysterical when I left the house. I walked ... I don't remember doing it, but I must have walked a mile to my dad's friend's house. I stayed with her for a few days and didn't call my dad to let him know where I was. His friend called.

At that point I had to go to work, so I was looking in the newspaper. I had lots of long, coal black hair. I was slim, like 120 pounds; I was real tiny. I'm only five three, not very tall. So I was looking in the newspaper to find a job and I see an ad that says "Exotic Dancers Wanted." I thought to myself "I'm exotic... long, dark hair." I figured I fit the bill. I didn't know what an exotic dancer was at that time. This was in Chicago. We were living on the south side then.

I answered this ad at this night club. It was

Age 25

in the daytime, and there were a bunch of women there. They dragged you up on stage in a pair of shorts and you walked around to the piano so they could see how you could dance. Well, I'd never had that problem, because I'd been a dancer all my life. I've always had very good rhythm.

So I get up on stage and I prance around. So did everybody else. And we're in this dressing room, and the lady who was running the show told us this really was strip tease, stripping. Some of the other girls said, "Oh, my goodness!" and they ran out.

So me and one other girl… I decided, "Why not? I've nothing to lose. It's a job. I get to do what I enjoy. I enjoy dancing. So I'll take a few things off." I was not shy. I was not bashful about that, so that's basically how I started as a dancer.

I didn't know what was in store for me. I had no idea. But I made a snap decision to do it, and I did it. And for over twenty years I had a wonderful vocation. It paid the bills. I made good money. Actually, back in '47—I guess it was '47—I was getting $200 a week, cash.

Ethyl never went back to her father's home. "I didn't care, really, because I felt he had his wife and I had my independence. I didn't need some snip telling me what to do, and what to wear, and where I could go."

Starting her new life, Ethyl Bronson now became known by her stage name, Ricci Cortez.

Ricci's career took her back and forth from Chicago to New Orleans with stops in between. In 1949, she was living with a man and got pregnant. They married, but it didn't last.

The S.O.B. didn't want to work so I finally kicked him out. When I had the baby, I divorced him.

While I was dancing [in Peoria, Illinois], I met a girl in the show who was gay. Now I was very straight. I didn't know anything about anything at that point. I'd had an experience with a woman in New Orleans before my daughter was born. But I thought that was just a fling… you know, a one-nighter.

Promotional pictures of Ricci at age 28

even performed there that night. At that party, she danced with Martha. She'd seen Martha in the bar before, but always with Ollie, so nothing came of it. Months later, when Martha came in the bar alone and Ricci found out Ollie was out of the picture, they began to see each other. They dated, but the relationship stayed casual.

> *When we went to Vegas and we were there for two days, she had her bed and I had my bed. … She treated me like the perfect gentleman, and I appreciated that. I never did sleep with her before we got together. It was something we just didn't do. I'm not that kind of a girl.*

Not long after, while they were having dinner with friends who were kidding Martha about Ricci, Martha declared, "Well, I'm crazy about the girl!" Their friends replied, "Then ask her to marry you." So, right there in the bar, Martha got down on one knee and asked her. That was the beginning of a twenty-year partnership.

Ricci and her brother continued to enjoy a good relationship over the decades. Once, while Ricci was working at the bar and

Ricci, 78, in Vegas at a burlesque reunion

her brother was visiting, he asked outright, "You running a lesbian joint here?" Ricci had never discussed her lifestyle with him, but he had met both Rita and Marion. "When he did find out about it, he was very cool with it. I was very glad that he did accept it, because my daughter has never really accepted it."

The relationship between Ricci and her daughter was difficult, at best. Her daughter had loved Marion, but she didn't seem to be okay with the fact that Ricci was a lesbian, or with her being a dancer. "Every time we went out, people would say to me, 'You look terrific.' She [her daughter] would cringe every time she heard that." Once her daughter was grown and gone, Ricci seldom heard from her unless she needed money.

When Ricci got into her early 80s, and Martha had died, she considered sharing housing with her brother, or moving into an assisted living facility.

> But I thought, "My house is paid for, my car is paid for, I have a small job three days a week... I'm able to work. And I can keep my home, and make my monthly bills, and I'm doing that." I've done that for almost a year now. I've gotten my head above water and aim to keep it that way.
>
> So I'd like to stay put. Because I love my home. I really do. It's mine. Like I said, it's paid for, it's new, it's not falling apart, it's not in disrepair. I don't live like a bag lady. I have my things that I want and need and like. So why move?
>
> I was in Las Vegas in 2006, in June, for the burlesque reunion, the old burlesque queens. I'm in the Burlesque Hall of Fame with my pictures. ... I didn't go [to the 2007 reunion] because my hip wouldn't let me. But I did go in '06, even though I had a stroke in January '06. I did go to Vegas in June and danced, performed there.

Ricci died in 2008, a few months after this interview.
Interviewer: Arden Eversmeyer
You can see a video of Ricci in action at the 2006 Burlesque Reunion at www.youtube.com. Use the keywords "Ricci Cortez."

Helen Cathcart

Born August 1916 in Arkansas
Interviewed in 1998 at age 82

False boobs, high heels and earrings.

An athletic girl raised in Arkansas, where sports played a huge role in everyone's life, if Helen wasn't in school she could be found on the local playground. Helen liked many sports, but as she matured she began to focus on basketball.

> *I didn't start playing basketball 'til I was about 16. I was a late starter. I was probably about 15 or 16, and we had this slumber party. And this girl, she was about three years older than I was, she said, "Well, I just think I'm gonna kiss you," and I says, "I just don't think you are." Of course, we ended up kissing, but I resisted, at least once.*
>
> *In high school, I had this woman that worked in the office. I don't know what she was, and I don't know what the conversation was about, or what was said or anything else. The only thing I remember that she said to me was, "To your own self be true, Helen." And she was straight, as far as I know, but she*

must have been telling me something that I already knew, and that she knew, too. I think it was pretty obvious that I was gay.

You didn't use that word then, but I don't think there was ever any question. In that time frame, the word "lesbian" was rarely used, and the word "gay"* hadn't even been invented yet.

The term most commonly used was "queer."

By the time she got out of high school, Helen excelled in both softball, playing shortstop, and basketball, playing guard. Both were tough positions, but not beyond her abilities. Back then, companies would sponsor ball teams, and Helen desperately wanted to be a part of those activities.

Helen knew her mother suspected her relationships with other girls.

I had made up my mind that was what I was gonna do. And I didn't want to tell my mother and daddy separately, so I caught them on the back steps at the house. I told them I had something I wanted to tell them; that I was gonna go to Galveston and play ball. Well, that didn't sit too well with my mother, and, of course, it didn't strike my dad.

She had, for some reason or other, got ahold of a few letters that I received from a woman who was on her vacation. And then she had overheard some telephone conversations. So she about decided there was something bad wrong with me.

Eventually, her dad relented and gave Helen enough money to make the trip.

When I got to Galveston I had 50¢, but I also had a place to stay, and a job. So I didn't need any money. I stayed at the YWCA and had three meals a day… until I got my first paycheck.

Helen played both basketball and softball for the American

Although the term "gay," defined as the antonym for "straight," had been used before then, it wasn't until the mid-20th century that it was commonly used to refer to homosexuals.

20-year-old Helen in uniform in 1936

National Insurance Company. But her "job" wasn't quite as straight-forward as it appeared. "When we were in town, we went to the office. If we didn't have to go get something physical, like rubdowns or something, then we were supposed to go to work. So as far as I'm concerned, it was at least semi-professional."

Helen traveled the country with her teams, playing everywhere from Madison Square Garden in New York to Soldier's Field in Chicago.

We were pretty good. And we traveled in cars. If it was summer time, I drove one car. We traveled in three cars in the summer time 'cause we had to have all the players.

I enjoyed the basketball years 'cause I was so numb-dumb. I didn't know from Shinola, so I just didn't have any worries, no problems. Just had a good time, and I enjoyed the playing.

In 1939

While the team was in New Orleans for a basketball game, Helen, her girlfriend, Doris, and their friends headed to a club where the gay men were known to hang out. "These three guys came in and sat between us. They said something, and I just turned my chair. I didn't want to fool with them; I wasn't looking for any trouble. Didn't want any."

As Helen returned from a trip to the bathroom, all hell broke loose. One of the men had reached over and put his hand on Doris' leg. Doris turned around and slapped him, and he slapped her back. Helen reacted, and the gay men who were in the bar had to come to their rescue.

I just lost it. ... I sort of vaguely remember hitting him. But I reached across that table and hit that son of a bitch. He sat on his butt and slid right across that baseboard. If we had not been in a gay club, we would have been in trouble. But those gay guys, they're fluffy and duffy and all that kind of stuff, but they can get down to it, too!

I quit [playing basketball] in 1940 because we lost the national championship. They were in the process of trying to rebuild our team. Most of the old [players] had quit and got married, or just flat quit. And I decided, "Well, I'm not gonna be doing that anymore." I decided I'd go to work for a living. That was a bad mistake.

World War II was just starting, and Helen took a series of jobs. After a brief stint supervising tabulations at the University of Houston, she began working at Cameron Iron Works, the same place as Doris, her lover. Helen stayed there for twenty-some years. It was a hard place to work, and things were always stressful. Toward the end of her stay at Cameron, they brought in someone new to take over the accounting department.

I kind of think that they decided they were gonna get rid of all the gay [employees]. Too many queers there. Now, that's my deduction. ... It could be my imagination ... on why they let me go, and why they let my boss [a gay man] go.

Finding a job at 50 years of age was a difficult task. Helen applied several places, and managed to get hired without having been interviewed. But when she showed up at work she was told, "If I had known you were as old as you are, I wouldn't have taken your application." After drifting around a bit, Helen took a job typing at Western Electric. She had first been offered a better position with the company, but turned it down. The interviewer had asked, "Would you have any objections to working for this man that is not as experienced and qualified as you are?" As Helen put it, "I'd just had a good dose of that!"

In one of her jobs, Helen was responsible for getting security clearances for employees. She had lent her typewriter to a young woman working there, and its return brought Helen to a turning point in her life.

> *Here she is about five-two or three, and was gonna bring my typewriter to me. [Helen was strong and almost 6 feet tall.] At that time I was wearing earrings and false boobs, and all that good stuff. And I go home and I said, "Man, I've had it! A little butch horse to carry my typewriter. I'm gonna get rid of all this stuff!" False boobs, high heels and earrings were a necessary part of life. Because if you didn't, honey, you just didn't have a good job. Women didn't wear pants.*

The same young butch woman came to talk to her later about her security clearance. She'd been discharged from the Army because of suspicions that she might be gay, and she was afraid of what a security check might bring about. If she quit to avoid the check, she worried it might make things worse for her situation in the Army. Helen helped resolve the young woman's dilemma by advising her that she could avoid the security check by quitting to go back to school full time.

Helen, age 48

Years later, the same woman approached Helen at a ball game. "I want to tell you how much I appreciate you helping me out." She had gone on to get her degree and was now teaching.

> *It's stuff like that, that bugs you! She said they [the Army] questioned her for six months. ... She ended up going to a psychiatrist, having to take treatments because of the trauma she went though then, from them trying to find out from her who was and who wasn't, and who was doing what.*

A lot of those women went through a bunch of crap like that. I never did join the Army, because I wouldn't have been in but one day and they'd have booted me right out the door!

Helen's family only played a peripheral role in her life once she had left home. She did have a twin, Herman, and a younger brother, Jim. Both were gay, but unlike Helen, they chose to live double lives. They had both married and had children, but carried on on the side. It caught up with her twin when he was in his mid-fifties.

"He got killed in Tulsa, Oklahoma. He picked up a guy and they went to this stadium … and this guy shot him and killed him."

Helen's younger brother, Jim, had also been stepping out on his wife.

He'd call me up and say, "Hey, Sis. I want you to talk to the prettiest thing in this world." And this guy would get on the phone. … I don't believe that Jimmy's wife was ever aware of any of this until Herman got killed. Then I think the bell began to ring in her little head.

Many women played important roles in Helen's life, but only a few of them qualified as relationships.

What I consider a relationship is someone that you've lived with for some length of time. If it's just a one-night stand, or a two-month stand, or something like that, forget it. I don't consider that a relationship. But when you've been through some of those nitty-gritties, then I consider that a relationship. And how many have I had of those? I would say three. That's not how many I've slept with… Like I always say, I'm not too good, but I last a long time.

Her first relationship had been Bonnie, the woman she went to Galveston with to play ball. They were together about four years, after which Bonnie married and had a child.

Bonnie unexpectedly dropped by to see Helen years later.

We talked a little while I was just standing there at the car [with her]. She said she was real concerned about her daughter.

She said, "You know, I think she is." And I says, "Well, if she is or if she isn't, don't worry about it. It'll all work out." And be damned if it didn't, if she wasn't right.

Next was her long-term relationship with Doris, the woman she fought over in the bar in New Orleans, and had worked with at Cameron Iron Works. This relationship lasted for 21 years. And then Helen and Dusty were together for over 17 years.

Helen and Dusty traveled extensively. "Gosh. We went to Canada, Mexico, Hawaii, Puerto Rico, Luxembourg, Spain, England, Innsbruck and Amsterdam." They often traveled with friends, specifically with two gay men.

After Helen had officially "retired," she had several more jobs. One of them was working at a local corner liquor store, to help out the owner. And when Helen was involved, even something as mundane as dusting shelves had its memorable moments.

This woman came in; she had a little boy with her. . . . I had seen her come in once in awhile, so I asked her how she was, and if I could help her. She said she just kind of wanted to look around, and I said, "Well, go help yourself." And she said, "Do you mind if ask you a question?"

I thought, "Holy shit. Here we come again." 'Cause that's the way they start out, that business with, "Oh, you remind me of somebody in The Well of Loneliness*". . . and I know exactly what they're getting to. So I said, "Oh, no. Go right ahead." She says, "Well, are you a man-she?" I said, "A what?" 'Cause I knew what she was talking about.*

Helen wasn't sure what the woman wanted, so she avoided admitting she was a lesbian. After apologizing if she'd hurt Helen's feelings, the woman went on to explain that she'd dreamed about Helen, and had even told her husband if she had the opportunity to be involved with a woman, she intended to try it. "I thought, 'Honey, you may be going to, but it ain't gonna be with me!'"

In her retirement, Helen also took on some remodeling that led to working as a contractor.

I always liked doing that. The first job I got, I was remodeling this woman's kitchen. And man, I bit off a hunk. "Holy man, am I gonna be able to do this?"... Painting wasn't anything. It was okay. I could handle that. But remodeling? I got into it and I got it finished, and it worked out to look real nice.

When she first started out she had done mostly painting but by the time she was done she'd taken on much more, even some roofing. (She roofed her own home three or four times.)

The way I learned is, if I called a plumber... I would watch them and talk to them, you know, ask them questions. I learned a lot from this plumber.

Eventually, all the years of drywall dust, paint fumes and smoking caught up with Helen. "I got sick, real sick. ... It started several years ago, but it just gradually got worse." She had quit smoking, and hoped that the symptoms would level off, but they didn't. Repeated bouts with pneumonia led to scar tissue in her lungs, and chronic emphysema.

It has slowed me down! You think about, "Well, I'm gonna get up, and I'm gonna do so-and-so." Well, you get up and do a little something, then you go "Whoosh!" Just winded. Have to stop and rest for a while.

Emphysema brought some changes to Helen's life, of course. She took things slower, and didn't go out as much. But the one thing it didn't change was her attitude. That same determination that served her well earlier in her life contributed to her gracious acceptance of her health limitations, and the high value she placed on the help others offered her.

Some things you just have to accept. And if you don't, then you go POOF! You make yourself unhappy and everybody around you, the people who care for you. You make it hard on them. I have to kind of space myself. I don't overload myself in one day. Tomorrow, I have to get a haircut. And I play poker tomorrow night.

Poker was a twice weekly event for Helen. These were not casual games. They often lasted four or five hours! The only concession she made, because of her emphysema, was to let someone else drive.

As things got harder for Helen to manage on her own, Dusty took on the role of caregiver. They had not been together as partners for years, but they continued to live next door to each other, and remained good friends.

> *I think that she does a wonderful job. And I think, as a taker, that you should accord certain courtesies toward the giver, because it's not easy for them either. ... You can't whine and bitch: "Well, I don't like this, and I don't like that, and you didn't do this, and you didn't do that." I ain't got time for that.*

Looking back at her life, and the importance of the women she'd been involved with, Helen offered some words of wisdom.

> *You sit and listen to people talk, and they think the more people they've slept with the better they are. But my contentions have always been that it's easy, if that's what you want to do—have two or three one-night stands a week. ... But I don't consider that as flattery. I don't know what that would do to a person's ego. 'Cause I've not slept with very many women in my life. I've been lucky — very, very lucky.*

Helen died in 1998.
Interviewer: Marguerite Shelton

Charlotte Doclar

Born April 1934 in Louisiana
Interviewed in 2002 at age 69

Southerners are just naturally affectionate.

"I was raised in a semi-Catholic background." Charlotte's mother, a very devout Catholic, had been excommunicated when she remarried, but that didn't keep her from raising Charlotte as Catholic as she could. Growing up, she was the only one in the family to not eat meat on Fridays, and she attended Mass every Sunday. And, of course, religion extended to her education.

I grew up in a Catholic school setting. I was a band member and a Girl Scout. I was a senior in high school and I didn't know what I was going to do with my life. I had thought about the telephone company, and you know, that kind of thing. That's what girls thought about in those days. Nursing and the telephone company, teaching and secretarial. I was so slow in school that they put me in the secretarial track. I got to fold a lot of letters and stuff envelopes. And I was supposed to learn how to type.

Charlotte, age two. (A surprising number of herstories contain photos similar to this one, and despite the geographic spread, many of the photos seem to be taken on the very same pony.)

It was about then that she found herself thinking about becoming a nun, but since she didn't go to church of her own volition, she worried she wasn't devout enough. "I only went on Sundays, and only because my mama pushed me to church."

As Charlotte started her senior year in high school, she also found herself confused about other feelings.

Age 11, with rosary in hand

I knew that I loved women by that time. Not that I loved them in a physical way, because that only came much later; but I always had girlfriends. I had a big crush on my P.E. teacher, who is now in the convent! We all had a crush on our band director.

There was a friend of mine, and she and I would go down in the basement and play games. They were those kinds of games where you really were kind of getting a little thing, a little kind of buzz, but we didn't know what it was. We would make up stories to tell each other. But it was only just the two of us. I don't know why somebody didn't suspect something.

Charlotte was clear about one thing: she didn't like men and never wanted to marry.

I was forced into going to the prom. My mother got my cousin to take me to my first prom. I really didn't want to go, but mama wanted to make the pretty dress for me. ... [I went to the other prom with] an older guy. And I was so afraid. We went out to this roadhouse where the smooching thing was going on, and I was just pasted to that right hand side of the car. I wasn't getting anywhere near him!

Finishing high school and feeling she didn't have any good alternative, Charlotte talked herself into entering the convent.

Age 18 with her mother

The first year in the convent, I just broke every rule. I didn't realize I was breaking every rule, but I did. I had a terrible Superior. She was really bad. I stayed in hot water, because I kept my bedroom door open, but I didn't know what it was. I mean, I was just being kind to people. They would come in my room and cry at night. So I got in trouble.

I had one friend, and she was really having a hard time. She wanted to leave the convent, and so she would come to my room at night. There was nothing sexual there at all yet. I was being a friend. But it was night time and … to break a silence is a mortal sin if you talk after night prayers. It's a mortal sin — a big sin. A mortal sin you go to hell for. … But I was breaking it all the time. She would come in and we would talk.

It was a struggle, but after two years of religious training in St. Louis Charlotte returned to her home town, New Orleans. At twenty, she was given a teaching position.

I was asked to take an eighth grade [class] because an older nun was dying of cancer. I was so big and tall, and these kids were terrible. That's the only reason that I got to take them. I did not know what I was doing.

The following year she was transferred to a nearby religious community where she taught for another five years.

> There are no locks on the doors in a convent. Very rarely will you find a lock. So you had to walk and open the door. I had to pass this older nun's room every night when I went visiting, and she reported it. Got in trouble there!
>
> So they sent me to Siberia, which was California in those days. I mean, it really was. I had a past. You have to understand. It was my renewal of vows year. You take vows for three years, and then you renew them for three years, and then you take them forever. It was in the interim, so they sent me to California, and California was really serious pagan-land.

Her stay in California was brief; she was sent to Texas, to the motherhouse for her convent.

> From then on, I was there [in Dallas]. But it was just like every place I went. You just gravitate to the woman who is a lesbian. … Sometimes it was a couple of people in one year. … I don't know how I did it. I don't know if it was because I was having a really good time while I was doing it, because it was hard. It really was. You fell in love and out of love so quickly, and no permanent relationships.

This went on for twenty-nine years before Charlotte revealed she was considering leaving the convent. The church sent her to a three-month retreat to give her time before she made her final decision. "And, of course, I found two women [at the retreat]. So that was that." She spent the following year working in the DC area in a gay Catholic ministry, all the while trying to come to a decision about leaving the convent. She just felt she couldn't stay.

> I was forty-seven when I left. At that time, my relationships were getting more and more heavy. Then I met some lesbians outside the convent and … I realized that I was really not being honest about who I was. I was just using the convent as a façade.

Going back to her motherhouse, Charlotte declared her intention to leave. "They accepted me for what I was and, in fact, they were very generous. They gave me a sabbatical, a year of doing nothing, in order for me to determine whether I wanted to leave, which was unheard of in those days." Using her sabbatical time to write her thesis, Charlotte graduated from Texas Women's University with a master's degree.

I was forty-seven years old, and had never made a decision on my own.... I knew I was a lesbian. I remember the first day I said the word. I was in Crowley, Louisiana, and I was lying on the floor in the lap of some young sister. We were listening to some kind of music, and I remember saying, "I think I'm a lesbian." And that word... I had the hardest time with that word coming out. Then after that, once I declared myself, then it became hard to be living in the community at the same time.

They gave me an opportunity to go to the first lesbian-nun retreat.... It was very crazy. We were running around Washington [D.C.] like we were crazy, screaming out of the window in the middle of the night, "I'm a lesbian and I love it!" Went to my first gay bar in Washington when we're all still in the convent.

We didn't know shit from Shinola, all those people, and a couple of cops walk into the bar. And we thought, "Oh, Jesus! We're going to get busted, and we're still in the convent!" And as far as the Catholic church was concerned, there were no lesbians in the convent.

During the sixties, we went out into the community. We helped the black people. We wanted to identify with the poor, identify with the black people. But we never identified with the gay people. The whole Catholic church and the nuns had an opportunity to bring the word lesbian up to a level where it wasn't looked down upon, but they missed that opportunity, because they didn't acknowledge the fact that it existed.

For herself, she even found nuns explaining away her behavior. "Oh, Charlotte. Don't worry about it, Sister John Ellen

[Charlotte's name while a nun]. You're just a southerner, and southerners are just naturally affectionate."

Starting a new life at age forty-seven definitely brought a new set of problems. Of course, there was no retirement money from the convent, but she was given three thousand dollars to get started. She used that money to get an apartment and a car.

Charlotte felt fortunate that, as a nun, she had spent the last few years living outside the convent and wearing street clothes. But she'd never had credit, and needed her father to sign so she could get a car to get to her job. With the help of an old friend and her master's degree, Charlotte immediately got a teaching position in Houston earning $19,000 a year.

In her new life, Charlotte gave an interview for a book entitled *Lesbian Nuns: Breaking the Silence.* It wasn't a best seller, but it was republished by Warner and sold in every Target and Walmart across the country. When it was republished for a broad audience, many of the names were changed so the women would be anonymous.

Because of the book, Charlotte came out to her niece, who encouraged her to tell her sister next. Charlotte explained her situation to her biological sister.

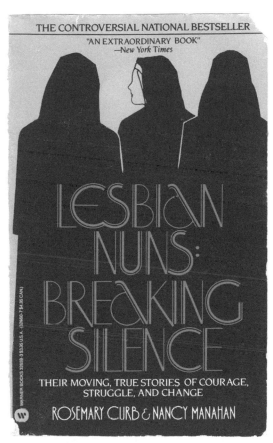

Original book cover 1985

Well, I wanted to let you know my story is going to be in a book, and that I'm a lesbian. I'm gay. She gave me the response you get every time you say it. "Oh, I knew it all the time." You know, baloney.

Charlotte brought her a copy of the book to read. "She was just so disappointed it wasn't more raunchy and sexy!"

She spent the first few years of retirement working as a volunteer among people with AIDS, but gave that up when the sadness became overwhelming. Now much of Charlotte's time is spent volunteering at church, only it's not the Catholic church; instead, it's a Unitarian Universalist church.

Asked if the people at the Unitarian church know she's a lesbian, Charlotte answers, "Oh, I'm definitely out. And it's a good feeling."

Charlotte continues to live in Texas.
Interviewer: Arden Eversmeyer

Sally Duplaix

Born in May 1936 in New Jersey
Interviewed in 2001 at age 65
Additional interview in 2008

Back then, that was considered 'crazy.'

Sally characterizes her early life as nearly ideal. She was born to a father who was a lawyer and a mother who was personal secretary to Charles Lindbergh. "For the first five years of my life I had no siblings. So I was an only child. And I must say ... I was really treated extremely well by my parents, and my grandparents, and my aunts and uncles." She now realizes many of the people around her had more money, but Sally knows her family was comfortable economically.

When I was born, there was a German nurse taking care of me. Later, we had a woman who lived with us. Her name was Mimi. She was my nanny. She was with me close to five years. And then the war came, and there were all kinds of changes, and other things happened.

About a year after my sister was born, a big thing

happened that really changed my whole life. ... My mother
developed breast cancer.

My mother had been fairly successful as a photographer's
model for advertisements. You saw her photo in magazines.
She was a very, very handsome woman, and had a lovely body.
[Then she] comes home from this radical, I mean radical,
mastectomy whereby every ounce of flesh down to the bone was
removed, and under the arm, everything.

Dealing with their mother's surgery was a trial for six-year-
old Sally and her one-year-old sister. In addition to the brutal
surgery, Sally's mother had to go through radiation that left her
burned, scarred, and thrown into early menopause. Although her
mother lived through the ordeal, it was extremely hard on Sally.

I lost my loving mother at six. ... I bore the brunt of her
frustrations, and her pain and anger. I took the brunt of it
because I was older. ... It did change our relationship ... and my
perfect childhood, this spoiled princess, everything I wanted ...

Sally's relationship with her father was the constant in her life
and helped guide her through her childhood. Dancing became an
important part of her life when she was seven or eight.

During that time, when I was living in Weehawken [New
Jersey], besides on Sundays driving into Manhattan to go to
Temple Emanu-El, ... I got very involved in dance, in ballet.
I was a fairly good student at ballet, so I was enrolled in the
School of American Ballet in New York City, with Victor
Balanchine. The school was connected with the New York City
Ballet Company.

I commuted into Manhattan alone to go to dancing
school several days a week. Even taking into consideration that
this was in a different day and age, taking a bus into the Port
Authority, and then a subway from Times Square, was a bold
act for a very young girl.

That was an exciting time ... it was exciting to be
performing [in the Nutcracker] with the New York City Ballet

Company, which actually happened ... and with my mother, for the most part, going to performances ...

New York City, with all it had to offer in dance, theatre and other arts, became Sally's second home. Her family continued to live in Weehawken, though they moved several times. During the summers, Sally was sent to camp.

Starting at a fairly young age, I'd say seven or eight, I'd spend the whole summer there. I loved camp. I guess I was homesick the first year or two, but I grew out of that pretty quickly. And I became sort of obsessed with horses ... I also did sailing, and canoeing, and swimming, and all the other things you do, and you also have friends. You make good friends, and you have the influence of the camp counselors.

At camp at age 15

Crushes on women camp counselors and school teachers became routine. Sally grew up going to weekly Temple, but her parents had opted to send her to a Protestant camp. Those early camp experiences also had a significant effect on her spiritual life.

In the beginning, I was the only Jewish child. Nobody knew. I don't think anybody knew. ... that's how I wound up becoming Protestant. It was the early childhood training. I was taught to fit in, to assimilate. My name didn't give me away. Nothing I said or did gave me away. And so this was the beginning of my becoming the perfect Protestant. But I think, in the beginning, when I realized, I was kind of astounded; I had never been the only anything before.

Camp affected Sally's life in other ways. "It was probably one of the influences that turned me into a lesbian. I'm not sure that that was the only influence, but it certainly was one."

As Sally neared high-school age, her family moved once again, this time a bit further into the country, where the schools were considered of a higher caliber. Even then, she continued to spend much of her free time in New York City. Not wanting to devote all of her efforts to ballet, Sally spent more and more time going to the theatre, ballet performances, classical music concerts and foreign films. She was also very involved in school activities.

Sally and her group of girlfriends were all fairly focused on grades and college, so interpersonal relationships weren't a big part of their lives.

> I had a group of friends; we were very close. They were all girls in this group. I mean, probably that's true of everybody when you're in high school. But I think, in my case, I didn't really date.... I was very late to mature. I was a late bloomer.... I was late to get a period, therefore I was late to develop breasts and I was late to have sexual thoughts about boys and things like that.
>
> I never had a boyfriend. I didn't go through all that stuff that most of my peers were going through. And I think a lot of it was because I really didn't develop until I was almost a senior. And by then I had recognized the fact that I was a lesbian. I knew it already by then. I had strong crushes.
>
> Not only was I having a crush on this one English teacher I spent a lot of time with, but obviously, in the summer, there were the counselors at the camp, my mother's friends, one of my aunts. I had crushes on all these women.
>
> I was spending a lot of time in New York doing various things and I remember starting to read and buy my first lesbian books back then, when I was still in high school.... I'd go to these adult book stores in the Time Square area. There were all these revolving racks of paperbacks.

Those books began Sally's prodigious collection of what later became known as "pulp" novels.

Where to go to college was the next decision. Aware that she had no interest in going to a co-ed school, Sally applied to Smith, Bryn Mawr and Vassar, and was accepted at all three. A strong French program swayed Sally to choose Smith. She had also felt drawn to the New England area. Sally planned to study French and spend her junior year abroad, but her plans were quickly derailed.

I left New York behind. I turned myself into my idea of a New England lesbian.... That's the beginning of my life, because before that freshman year at Smith nothing out of the ordinary happened to me. I was pretty safe. I was protected. My real life began back then, in 1954-'55 ... and then my sexual awakening.

That freshman year, I met someone. I met a woman who was on the faculty. She [Jean] was a visiting professor [from Spain]. She spotted me, and that was the first lesbian that I'd ever met. A real lesbian. Because other people that I'd had crushes and fantasies about were not. This was the first, and she spotted me, and she actually proceeded to seduce me.

It was intense, because it was my first relationship of any kind. And I'd been waiting all those years, and I was now nineteen going on twenty, and discovering love; and it was a very intense and very emotionally charged situation. I went a little nuts in love. You know. This love, this all consuming ... and I can't think about anything else, and it changes your life.... It actually changed my life in more ways than one, some of which were not so good, and some of which were good.

Being with Jean that year ... it was very dangerous.... A student and a faculty member! ... That "L" word at Smith, in Northampton back in 1954, was not, I repeat, not cool, and we knew it. So there was a lot of sneaking around, sneaking into her room, breaking curfews, lying, danger of being caught. Everything was charged. So in the end it was ... part of the excitement, I think, was the danger of the whole situation.

Jean went back to Spain, and Sally entered a summer course that immersed her in French. "For me, that summer was a summer of real sexual exploration, because she [Jean] had awakened the sleeping giant which had been buried for a long time."

*All my growing up, it had been buried. I had never ever kissed
a boy, I had never necked. I had never done any of that stuff. So
there I am in Middlebury, and I'm looking pretty good, and I'm
meeting people, and I'm falling in love.*

That summer, Sally became engaged to a fellow student, a
Russian man who had lived in France. He had family in South
America. Together they traveled to Columbia for the holidays, and
she saw, for the first time, how people lived in other parts of the
world. The relationship didn't last, and Sally returned to Smith,
where life became even more confusing.

*I guess I was caught in my room with my roommate, in a
sexually compromising position … I was referred to the college
shrink at the time. I was referred because my behavior was
quite "unacceptable."*

The psychiatrist suggested that Sally receive some kind of
therapy, and her parents were told that she was having a nervous
breakdown.

*I don't know if it was defined as a nervous breakdown or just
mania and depression. But I did go that summer. They found
me a psychoanalyst in New York City, where I commuted in five
days a week to see the shrink.*

*Then, at some point, I don't remember the exact order, the
shrink recommended that I go to this place which was a very
classy upscale place in New Canaan [Connecticut], which dealt
with people who had problems.*

Sally was fortunate to have been placed in a nice facility, and
to have a supportive family. Even so, things didn't go well.

*We had sessions with the analyst … I continued with my lesbian
stuff. … we're back in 1956 and I'm going around telling people
how proud I am, and happy I am, and I think it's the most
wonderful thing in the world that I'm a lesbian.*

*Well, back then that was considered crazy. That was
considered serious crazy. You had to be. You had to absolutely*

be weird to talk like that, to think like that, to not cover it up and be ashamed. It was too easy for me to tell people, I think, because I was so proud of it; I thought it was the greatest thing in the world. Well, it wasn't. ... So I was sent from there. They couldn't handle me, they said, because they didn't have strong enough treatments there. This was too much like day camp for recovering alcoholics, or whatever. So I was sent to a private mental hospital.

This was a real mental hospital, but, as they kept on reminding us, a private hospital where we were treated a lot better than if we had been in a state asylum. ... That was the threat: if you don't behave, you could end up in [the state asylum].

Well, this was serious business. There were medications. There were two kinds of shock treatments. There was electric shock in the morning, and insulin coma in the afternoon.

Here I am, little Miss Spoiled valedictorian, Smith College student, locked up in this cuckoo place ... complete with torture. I mean this is awful stuff happening. This is not like Silver Hill, with recovering alcoholics. This is one step from lobotomy. I was there from August to sometime in December. ... It was like daily horror stuff going on.

Sally was finally released, but not because they considered her cured. "I really wanted out of there. They released me because my parents promised that they would put me under the care of a psychoanalyst in New York."

Life back in New York included therapy sessions, but it also provided some breathing room for Sally to begin rebuilding her life. She started taking classes at Columbia University, studying Spanish and Portuguese. She also went to work for a French company.

In 1958, Sally was hired by Pan Am Airlines as a stewardess, flying in and out of South and Central America on a regular basis. It wasn't on her route, but she also managed to visit San Francisco.

"The only people I knew in San Francisco were Phyllis Lyon and Del Martin, because of *The Ladder* [a periodical whose cover

her photos later graced twice], because I'd been subscribing to it."
Phyllis and Del, pioneers in lesbian rights, showed Sally around,
and insisted she stay with them for Thanksgiving. "It was probably
the first time in my life I was ever in a home owned by two women,
with other lesbians."

Back in New York, life also began to include a wider circle
of friends, gay and straight. Sally also was now working for the
French-speaking owner of Golden Press Books, as his executive
assistant. "Somewhere along the line I met his stepson ... and
we started to date." She was upfront with Michael about her past
affairs. After they had lived together for six months, Sally's family
urged them to marry, so they did.

Life was grand for a while, filled with excitement, theater
openings and other cultural events. Then they took a trip to
Vermont to meet Michael's biological father.

> His father had a girlfriend, an older woman, a lovely older
> woman with gray hair. And I fell in love with her. So that was
> the end of the marriage.
>
> That's when I really started my lesbian life in New York
> City, meeting lesbians through [an old friend].... There were
> two ways to meet in New York. There was the bar scene,
> different kinds of bars, but still bars. And then, once you met
> people, there was a whole world of private parties.

Soon, Sally was in her first "real" lesbian relationship, with
Ginny Dunbar. Three years into their life together, Sally and Ginny
took a summer off to travel Europe, before they moved to New
England. They bought a car in France and drove everywhere, seeing and tasting everything.

Coming back to settle in Rockport, Massachusetts, was
culture shock. Since she was geographically close enough to her
former life, Sally relied on old friends for a social circle, "We
celebrated holidays together, we celebrated birthdays together, we
spent summer vacations together. That was our little world."

Jobs in the area were scarce unless you wanted to work in the
fishing industry, so Sally took up modeling for artists at the local
art school for a few years. Looking for more opportunities, Sally

and Ginny next moved to Boston, where Sally could go back to school. In 1970, Sally graduated summa cum laude with a degree in psychology.

> *It was a thrilling time [the 60s] for somebody like myself, who was in my thirties by that time, to be going to school. But while this was all happening, I broke up with Ginny.*
>
> *Immediately upon graduating, I went to graduate school [Simmons] for a master's degree in library science, which started my adult life and career, and it was kind of the beginning of a whole new part of my life. ... When I was a student there in 1971, I remembered that my first lover, the woman who had been the teacher at Smith, had a sister very close to her in years. And I remember her talking about her, and the fact that the sister was a teacher at Simmons College in the undergraduate school. So while I was there I looked her up.*
>
> *[Ginnie Bratton] decided to have me come over to her home. ... I went to her home for dinner and began what was to become my peak, or prime, lesbian relationship with the person that I probably loved the most of any of the women that I was involved with.*

Sally earned her master's degree, and worked for several years learning practical applications for what she'd been taught in school, building a reputation in the library system. Sally took directorship of the library in a nearby community, turning around the troubled system. She held that position for nine years. Sally subsequently secured a coveted position as director of a prestigious private library in Providence, Rhode Island, a job which led to several wonderful opportunities. During her tenure at the Providence Athenaeum, she learned a great deal about conservation of rare books and other bound materials, and became their public spokesperson, frequently providing interviews for television and print media.

Commuting from Boston quickly became untenable, so Sally and Ginnie bought a condo halfway between their two jobs. Whenever they weren't working, they packed up their dog, two cats, and gear and headed to Chatham on Cape Cod.

The year before they met, Ginnie had purchased five acres of property on the Cape, with a small cottage. It was idyllic — until the unthinkable happened.

Ginnie Bratton in 1975

There was no electricity. There was no running water. You can't have running water without electricity. There was no phone. There was nothing but this adorable, hand-built cottage.

It was a beautiful August day in 1986. We were in the second week of our two-week stay with all the animals and everything. It was in the morning. We still didn't have a telephone... we did have electricity... we did have running water, but we did not have a phone. Because of the lack of a phone, I needed to cancel an appointment Ginnie had made. ... She was planning to retire the following year. She was 61 years old, and was taking early retirement. She had spent 36 years at the same college, teaching. ... I had to go out and make a phone call because she didn't feel well and try to cancel the appointment. ... When I came back, she was dead. There I was with no phone, and she was dead. And I was alone, and I had to deal with it, had to get help.

I went down to the hospital, and there was this really good social worker there who sat and talked with me, and obviously figured it out. I've always been out, so there was no way I was hiding how important this person was to me.

That night when I got home [the Boston area], I got a phone call from that woman at the hospital, who wanted to know if I was okay. That has stayed with me because it was such a non-homophobic thing to do. ... [She] obviously understood the relationship, and rather than being negative about it ... I've heard these horror stories about people who couldn't even get in to visit their dying partners ... this woman called me to make sure I was okay.

What followed was almost as difficult. Ginnie had not been out about her sexuality at the college, and had almost no family.

At school, all of her friends, long-term friends from the faculty and administration, none of those people had ever dealt with me before. Didn't know I was even there, or chose to ignore it.... I was set up in the receiving line as the widow, as the grieving widow in the line, with the president of her college... They acknowledged my presence, even though she'd been closeted. So that, for me, is the irony. She was outed at death. It kind of left a funny taste in my mouth because, in some ways, it was hurtful to me that she didn't include me in on that part of her life when she was alive.

Sally continued commuting to her job, but after a year or so she realized it didn't make sense anymore ... she no longer needed to live mid-way between her job and Ginnie's. Sally moved, but life didn't get much easier, and she finally had to quit working.

I never really recovered from her death. It took me a long, long time. I would be driving the car to work, and I'd start bawling. Tears would be rolling down my face. I was driving down Route 95, and crying, sobbing in the car. I couldn't believe what had happened. Well, okay, we had a funeral. We had a memorial service.

My family was very supportive. They were really worried about me. And what happened was, I was going through her stuff, trying to pay her bills and organize, because I guess I was serving as kind of the executor.... She didn't even have a lawyer.

What happened was she had written a bunch of holographic wills, handwritten wills, and stuffed different wills in different places. And every time I'd open a drawer, out would pop a new will.... They were not legal wills, because they were not done by a lawyer. In Massachusetts, a holographic will is not a legal will unless it is certified.... Basically, she had left me on the life insurance, on part of her pension. ...

The main thing was the property on the Cape, and it was clear in everything she wrote that I was to inherit the property.

Between what she had inherited and her own pension, Sally took an early retirement so that she could focus on herself.

Sally decided to venture out once again a few years later and she wrote to several interesting-sounding women in Golden Threads. One woman, Deedy, stood out as someone who shared her love of animals, bird-watching, and the Cape.

A relationship developed between Sally and Deedy, and they began to spend their shared time at the cottage in Chatham with friends. "Everybody started coming and visiting us because we had this ideal place on the Cape. People would come and pitch their tents, and spend weeks here. It was almost like tent city here, lesbian tent city."

All the women coming and going, and a lack of plumbing, led to a crisis that motivated Sally to build a full-fledged house on the land. After navigating the arduous process of building on land that demanded close attention to the environmental impact, Sally decided on two buildings. She preserved the hand-built cottage, and had it moved to a new location on the land, and had a new home built. Now she not only had a house with all the amenities, but a nearby cottage that could be rented out to friends and other lesbians to provide supplemental income.

Sally with friend, Laurel (on left)

Meeting Deedy brought Sally's activism back into the forefront. She had always been involved in various ways, but now she had some-one with similar ideas and interests to spur her on. Together they were involved in help-ing organize a women's music festival. When they learned about a planned lesbian conference on a national level, they knew they had to go.

What happened was I discovered that there was an organization called OLOC [Old Lesbians Organizing for Change]. ... It was discovering this whole new world for us; people who were more contemporaries. Because our crowd, except for one or two people, were mostly much younger. They were people in their twenties and thirties, and here I was in my fifties, and Deedy was in her sixties. We really wanted friends of our own age.

Two years later, Sally and Deedy found themselves boldly taking part in the March on Washington. "The TV reporters had the video camera going, and Deedy's right out there at the front of the march, and they focused on her. She was saying, 'Two, four, six, eight. How do you know your grandma's straight?'" They found out later that the clip was run that night on the NBC Nightly News with Tom Brokaw.

Deedy had become involved in the OLOC leadership almost immediately, and as soon as Sally was old enough (the group is limited to 60 and older), she joined their Steering Committee.

Books, especially books about lesbians, had always been important to Sally, starting back in the 50s with her collection of pulp fiction. She'd continued collecting what she could, but retirement and space allowed her to pursue this passion more seriously. "What I'm collecting now, and I'm again trying to be pretty thorough, is just OLOC material. It is strictly material by and about lesbians over sixty."

Developing and strengthening the local community on the Cape was also important to

Deedy and Sally

schools] to squeeze four years of college in! ... I was always
working towards some degree. I changed my major so many
times, but I was always working toward something.

Sixteen-year-old Tre was determined to make enough money
to start out at TSCW, and spent her first summer after high school
selling Bibles door-to-door in Dallas. "Ten dollar Bibles, and I
would not let anybody not buy a Bible!" Tre laughs. To supplement
that income, she also took a night job in an ammunition factory.

You know how the government gives you a test to work for
them? ... I made such a high score that they called me in to go
to downtown Dallas to meet the big old, huge guy who worked
for the Corps of Engineers. ... He said he just wanted to meet
me to see what kind of person could make that high a score.

Undeterred by her young age, Tre was given the position of
Chemical Warfare Service Inspector in a bomb factory. ... "Here I
was, this little gay girl who knew she was gay, running the lives of
all these people!" Between the two jobs, "I made enough money to
put myself through my freshman year of college."

Tre passed by a bookstore on her way to and from work at the
factory, and a certain book in the window caught her attention.

There were a hundred books, all of them just alike, and they
were called Diana, A Strange Autobiography. *I went in and*
bought the book. I took it home. It was all about this love
affair between this woman and these other women. I called my
mother and I said, "Mom, I am a homosexual, just like these
women in this book." She said, "I always wondered when you
were ever going to find out."

All those years she knew. She never told me. I never knew
anything about it, never heard the word "homosexual," never
heard the word "lesbian," never heard the word "gay." I was still
that nice, sweet, little innocent child.

That was when I was sixteen, and then I went off to
college, probably three weeks later, and went crazy!

Whoa. Five thousand women. Not enough time!

Even when Tre had started college and was involved with other women, being a lesbian was never named.

People were afraid. I remember I told the woman who was going to marry my brother that I was gay (by that time we were using the word) and ... she was afraid of me.

I told her, "You just let me sleep in your room tonight and I'll show you I'm not going to attack you. Just because I'm gay doesn't mean I'm attracted to you, or going to attack you." So she let me sleep in her room to prove to her that I was not going to molest her or bother her. This is a big deal ... straight women didn't understand this at all. They were scared that someone was going to come after them.

At TSCW, Tre spent most of her time taking the courses she wanted to take, instead of those that were required. Good grades were not a high priority.

I made such bad grades, they would put me on scholastic probation; and the next semester I had to make it up, to make good grades, so I could stay in college for another four months. Then I would make it, and I'd get on scholastic probation again.

The summer after her freshman year, Tre started out working at a girl's camp in Colorado. "The woman that owned the camp ... would have strange men there all night long, and I just didn't like that a bit. I thought it was terrible that she did this. Being the 'little puritan' that I was, I just quit." After a brief stint in Wyoming on a dude ranch, Tre went back to North Carolina, where she had family.

Visiting nearby Washington, DC, Tre fell in love with a female cousin, and stayed and worked in that area for a year before heading back to TSCW. However, the money ran out before she finished her sophomore year, so off she went again.

I went to New York with these friends of mine, one of whom had been kicked out of college for being gay. They never kicked me out of college for being gay, because I was this nice sweet girl who went around telling everybody that I was gay, and they didn't do anything to me. But they kicked out almost 500 girls that year.

    I'm telling you, it was terrible. But they never got me.... You couldn't drink, you couldn't drive a car, you couldn't do this, you couldn't do that, and if you were gay and they found out, boy you got kicked out so fast. Just think of the lives of the people they ruined.

Living in New York was much more expensive than going to college, but Tre managed to do both. "I worked for some sheet metal guys.... but I mostly worked for doctors. I transcribed their records ... off of wax cylinders." Tre had had several pre-med courses, and knew the vocabulary, so she liked that job. She had her first cup of coffee, her first beer, and her first cigarette while living in Greenwich Village at age 19.

You didn't have to worry about being gay when you were on the street. You just worried about being gay when you were in the bar. You couldn't wear as many as two articles of male clothing, or you'd be arrested... you know, like a shirt or a pair of pants, jeans or anything.

Tre and her cousin

Taking advantage of another opportunity, Tre apprenticed herself to a sandal maker while living in New York. She then decided she'd take off for Europe and bicycle everywhere she could. However, she made the mistake of calling her mother first, who said, "You are NOT." Changing her plans slightly, Tre took the idea in another direction.

Tre (on the right) with a friend in Greenwich Village in 1948

"I got on my bicycle and rode all the way [from New York City] to Dallas. Then I went back to TSCW again." Along her travels, Tre (along with a business partner) set up sandal shops. She even had one in her dorm room. "I always had work, I always had a way to support myself."

Tre moved back and forth across the country, often traveling hundreds of miles on her old Schwinn three-speed bike, and periodically returning to TSCW to take a few more classes. During one of her stays in Texas, Tre bought a piece of property and started building a house. But her family managed to talk her into moving to California, partly to be near them, and partly to get Tre away from a relationship with a married woman. Tre fell back on her medical transcription skills in California. She even worked as faculty at Stanford, teaching pre-med classes for the doctor for whom she was transcribing records.

> *Then I decided I had to get married because I had to have a baby. My brother was in the Marines, and he had this buddy I started going out with. I went down to spend Christmas with my brother in LaJolla, and Eddie was there. I told Eddie that I thought we should get married. I wanted to have a baby.*
>
> *So we rushed off to Yuma, Arizona and got married. That sucker; I gave him five or six shots [at impregnation], and he shot blanks every time. ... I didn't get pregnant, but I thought, "Boy, this is no good. This is not working."*

Married life, or at least this marriage, didn't suit Tre's temperament at all.

> *My husband would not let me speak to another person, male or female. He was so jealous. We had this little 85-year-old land-lady. We lived on the third floor of a house in San Francisco, and the back steps needed to be painted, and he wouldn't let me go back to work. ... He was in the Marines, [and away from home] so I told her I would paint those back steps.*
>
> *I was right at the very bottom, and he came home and he stood up on the third floor ... and he said, "Did I tell you you could paint these steps?" I said, "No, you didn't." He said, "You*

don't do anything without my permission, and you do not do anything without asking me. You get up here." I got up there. I said, "I am leaving."

Two and a half months and fifty dollars later, Tre was divorced.

After quite a bit more rambling and several more jobs, Tre went back to San Francisco, where she ran one of her sandal shops. She also purchased three lots for $25 each at Yosemite. The rumor was the government was going to confiscate any land left bare, so Tre built a cabin straddling two of her lots. When the government did step in to take the land, Tre, with the help of a lawyer, managed to get some money and to keep the use, but not clear ownership, of the cabin for as long as it was there. Tre wasn't surprised when the cabin mysteriously burned down. When it did, the government simply took the land.

Having had a taste of building, Tre began another job.

I worked at the lumberyard, and I really enjoyed that. Then I thought I deserved a raise. I asked them for a $25 raise. After all, I was the inside salesman, which was a big deal. I was on the phone talking to a couple hundred people a day selling carloads of lumber. I was learning everything there was to know about hardwood, softwood, every aspect of construction.

At 65 years old

When the lumberyard wouldn't give her the raise, Tre quit the job and headed back to school. After she left, they had to hire three people to replace her.

Those three people were just giving them fits! They begged me, called me, begged me to come back. Finally they said they would give me a hundred dollar raise if I would. ... I should have stayed in school but ... in those days, that was a lot of money.

Never one to stay in one job or one place for long, Tre eventually got her degree and teaching credentials, and taught at two different school districts in California.

"I loved teaching. I loved it so much that I didn't think they should pay me for it!" Getting into the school systems during a time when teachers were highly valued, Tre stuck with it.

"I had a wonderful, wonderful fifteen years teaching, and I really enjoyed it." But as the times changed, people cared less and less about the quality of a teacher, and Tre felt it was time, yet again, to move on.

Tre had started building another house during her last few years as a teacher. "I realized that this [building] was where the fun was." Once she started, she couldn't stop. Tre earned a bit of publicity in the '80s when it became known she had an all-woman construction crew.

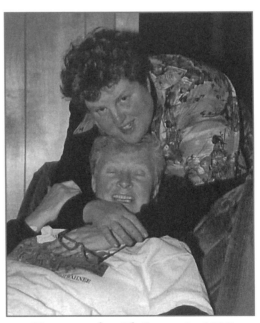

Tre, seated, with Susan in 1993

I got publicity because women hadn't started being in the trades yet. This was in 1984. I was in People *magazine. ... I did that, and I think it started a lot of other women to think that they could do something like that. They didn't have to sit at a computer, they didn't have to be a secretary, they didn't have to be a teacher, they didn't have to be stuck in a position they didn't enjoy; they could go out and work on their own.*

At the time we were graduating from college there really was no future outside of being a secretary, or a teacher, or a nurse. ... Women should have been the people, the architects, who designed houses. ... Women have always been the people using the end product. They should be the people planning those things.

Fifty-four houses later, and 72 years old, Tre says, "I really, really love building. It is a challenge, I learn something every day. Every day you have something new to conquer. ... Nothing tickles me any more today than putting on my overalls."

Tre continues to live (and build houses!) in California, where her well-traveled Schwinn bike hangs in the garage.
Interviewer: Arden Eversmeyer

WHEN THESE WOMEN TALK NAILS, THEY AIN'T TALKIN' POLISH

The workers who amble across the redwood-fringed construction site lugging huge 6-inch by 6-inch by 25-foot beams and hammering together the wooden frame of a restaurant don't look much like hard hats: All seven are wearing earrings, gold necklaces and a tasteful touch of eye makeup. These are the women of Tre-Lee Construction of Mariposa, Calif., a strikingly successful all-female building company owned and operated by Tre Ford, 56, and Lee Gallagher, 37.

Since 1974 Tre (short for Tresse) and Lee have erected 22 buildings in this sleepy former mining town and they are now working on their first commercial building, a 3,000-square-foot New England-style showpiece known as Tink's Little Acre. Already admiration for Tink's has garnered the women nine new construction jobs. "Everybody thinks it's the most beautiful building in town," says Ford. Equally impressive, the women have even won the heart of Fred ("the Godfather") Bardini, 76-year-old owner of Mariposa's largest shopping center. "I always had the feeling that women belonged in the kitchen," Bardini admits, "but they make a lot of the men contractors look foolish because of how precise and finished their jobs are." Their price looks nice too. While male counterparts get $30 an hour, Tre-Lee charges only $10.

"Anyone can do this," claims Ford. "Just remember you're only nailing one nail at a time." In fact, the only on-the-job hazard the crew acknowledges is weight gain. "You eat to keep up your energy," Gallagher says. Nancy Wessels, 27, maintains that "the only difference between us and men is that we use finesse rather than brute strength."

Indeed Tre-Lee is a prime example of brains triumphing over brawn. Ford (lower right in photo), who has a degree from California State University at Chico, is a member of MENSA, the organization for those with IQs in the top 2 percent. Gallagher (above Ford) is a graduate of Miss Porter's School (which polished Jackie O) and has a master's degree in history from the University of California at Santa Barbara. Wessels (top) has a masters in sports medicine, Pat Stacy (left, top of ladder), 45, is an ex-nun and Harvard alumna and Sandy Bloom (lower left), 31, is a housewife.

Ford learned her construction skills "by reading a lot of books" and working in a lumberyard. The daughter of a Tulsa painting contractor, she met Gallagher, the Menlo Park-bred daughter of a Shell Oil executive, in 1970 when both were teaching elementary school in Cupertino. After they built themselves a 2,500-square-foot weekend retreat in Mariposa, Tre-Lee "just kind of happened," Gallagher says. It became full-time and the house became year-round in 1980.

"We are a springboard for some and an ultimate career for others," Ford says of her unusual firm, to which no men have applied. "I'm not competing with any man. It's just that if a woman feels like doing something like building, she should be able to do it." □

Photograph by Steve Smith/Wheeler Pictures

This People *magazine article (dated October 1, 1984) profiling Tre's all-woman building crew reconnected Arden Eversmeyer with Tre more than 30 years after they'd had met at Texas State College for Women. Tre is on the lower right.*

Jennie Gates

Born September 1927 in Texas
Interviewed in 2000 at age 73

Be yourself and be whatever you are.

When I was twelve, I had a next door neighbor who was so cute. She was the same age, and we would always... so childish ... we would always say we loved each other, but it was kind of play talk. And then we'd take a nap together fully clothed, and we would pretend we were boy and girl friend, and one would be on top of the other. You know, the proper moves, but not really doing anything.

Then when I was 15, I had this girlfriend who lived down the street from me ... and we would spend the evening together at her house or mine. Well, after dark, one would walk the other halfway home, and we would say all these funny little kid things like, "Oh, God. I wish I could spend the night with you!"

There was another woman in school, a young woman, at least a couple of grades higher than me. I had a girlfriend. We didn't know anybody. Typical story: we didn't know anybody else like us existed, but we were enjoying each other so much. So this Catherine, one time she said, "I have a friend and we like to just drive around the city. Would you guys like to ride with us some time?" So she comes and picks us up and we're on a ride around downtown.

We're in the back seat, kind of necking a little bit, and next thing I know she has driven into this wooded area, God knows how far from houses. We're in the back seat ... necking up a storm. All of sudden we discover those two are in the front hanging their chins over the back of their seats watching us. And they go, "I knew it, I knew it. I knew we weren't the only ones." So then there were four of us. ... You had to be so daggone careful. I don't remember how it happened, but I discovered my first gay bar. I don't even know how.

When I was 15, I was still in high school. I was an elevator operator in the Rusk Building in downtown Houston. I don't think it even exists anymore. This was during the war when nylons were so hard to get — they were impossible, pretty much — but I had one pair of nylons, and they had such runs that there was more run than there was stocking. But I was required to wear those to work and that's what I did.

Jennie realized she was in a go-nowhere position, and, as soon as she got a chance, she went to work for an oil company as a well-spotter. "I thought, 'Oh, good. I'll be out in the field.' Wrong! Wrong! Wrong! ... My job was to find the proper map and to locate that [oil] well on that map, and put in the mathematical location. That was a stupid, stupid job." There were a few special perks of the job, however. Jennie met lots of interesting women and, when she worked on weekends, she could dress casually.

On Friday night, we'd be together and drinking, and doing all this bad stuff. Here I am just 17 years old. And I'd go to work on Saturday in my "boy" clothes. My brother was in the Navy, and I was wearing his drapes [pants] and his shirts. Couldn't wear his shoes; my feet weren't big enough. But I would have if I could have. And I'd go to work in that. ... I always had a girl friend; I always had two or three at a time.

I had one who worked upstairs in that same building and we would meet in the stairwell and neck. Stupid! Well, my boss learned about that. I had only been there a few months when he called me in one Saturday, when I was in my brother's boy clothes, and he gave me this very sweet, very understanding lecture about how I was presenting myself. He didn't think it would be a good idea for me to continue to work there. So I'm fired from my first real job for being a dyke.

Someone loaned Jennie the book *The Well of Loneliness* while she was still in high school.

17-year-old Jennie

Probably somebody who was trying to find out if I was gay or not. So I took that book home and I would read it at night. Mother went to sleep earlier than I did. I had my own room and had my door shut and the light on reading. When I got through reading it for the night, I'd just hide it under my mattress. And, dang it, I came home [from the bar] one time, two o'clock in the morning, and Mother was sitting on the commode, lid down, reading The Well of Loneliness *from where my bookmark was.*

Well, it happened to be right in the middle of some wild party, and the worst part that she could possibly have read to try to get anything good out of this book. If she'd started from the front, she might have understood. But no.

We had a knock-down, drag-out fight that night. My glasses got broken. We were just whamming away at each other. She hated that I was doing that, that I was interested in that. And it never got any better.

Jennie loved women's softball, and went to every game she knew about.

I'd take the bus to ball games. Annie S. used to say, "Well, come on home with me. It's too late for you to go home on this bus by yourself." So I'd go home with her. Now it's too late to take the bus home, so I'd stay overnight. She lived in a garage apartment, no telephone. My mother didn't know where I was. I didn't care that she didn't know where I was. I'd be home sometime. It never occurred to me that she'd be worried. Thought she wouldn't even notice.

So the next morning the landlady came knocking on the door. "Is there a Jennie here? I had a phone call from somebody saying Jennie's her daughter." Oh, Lord. Mother had reported me as a missing person to the Houston police. On a Sunday morning, in my butch clothes that I wore to the ball game, I had to go to the downtown police department and report myself not missing, whereupon I got about a 30 minute lecture on how to treat my mother, and how not to do things like this to my mother. Not a word about how I was dressed, thank God.

After one softball game, a group of the women were going to a bar together.

They were all going to go, but I knew that I shouldn't go because I was only 17 years old, and I knew I couldn't go there. I went on home. Thank God I went home, because I was told later that the place was raided, and that all the girls were lined up against the wall, flashlights shone on them, mostly on their feet. Anybody that had on boy's shoes was hauled off. So thank goodness I didn't go.

Jennie decided she needed to get a "real job," took a six-week course learning how to use Burroughs calculators and was hired by the Southern Pacific Railroad.

The first week I was there, the first day I was there, as I was introduced to people, they said, "You sure do remind us of Helen." At this time, I am 19.... Well, Helen came back from

her vacation, and I could see why they said that. We didn't
look a thing alike, but we dressed the very same way. We both
wore saddle oxfords and socks, and had on gathered skirts and
blouses. We stayed together for five years. ... She and I had
double-dated with my brother and his girlfriend. They ended
up getting married and, kind of, so did we.

Jennie quickly grew to hate her job at the railroad, where
she had to work at a frantic pace for half of the month and sit and
pretend to be busy the other half. Bored and restless, Jennie knew
she had to make another change, and she began taking drafting
courses on weekends.

After five years at Southern Pacific, I told my lover that I was
going to get this other job at Brown & Root and she said, "Well,
you know what I've always told you: If you ever stop working at
Southern Pacific, we're through." We were through.

In retrospect, Jennie thinks it might have been because her
girlfriend wouldn't be able to keep an eye on her. The position at
Brown & Root, making technical drawings for the engineering
firm, was another entry-level job, but Jennie was finally doing
something that interested her. When the company ran out of work
for the draftsmen three years later, she was laid off. Jennie, now 26,
saw this as her chance to start fresh elsewhere.

"I had always wanted to move to California, because I heard
it was ... well, everybody knew what California was like. In Los
Angeles, everybody could be gay and nobody cared." Jennie moved
to San Francisco, took a job as a draftsman, and began to develop a
social life. It only took that one year working as a draftsman there
to convince Jennie she needed more schooling.

I was going to study engineering. When I went into junior
college, that's what I told them, and that was fine. I took all
the basic courses for that, and got my [AA] degree. ... So then I
transferred to University of California Berkeley.

Jennie had quit her draftsman job after a discussion with
her boss. When asked what she planned to study in college, her

boss told her, "Well, don't come back here and ask for a job. We don't hire women engineers." She found out her former employers weren't the only ones discriminating against women.

> *Several times during my two and a half years [in college], I got remarks about women in men's fields. In a chemistry class, for instance, every time I asked a question they would laugh at me. I was the only woman in the class. And they would laugh up a storm at me for a stupid question, like "dumb woman."... Constantly, remarks like this.*
>
> *I decided I cannot fight this battle. I'm not a strong enough person to go into a field where I'm not wanted and fight this battle forever. So I'll change my major to French and go into teaching instead. Broke my heart to do that, but I did that.*

Jennie had to work hard to put herself through college. Although her mother had always said she'd help her, she never did. "I went to school and worked at the same time. Then I'd quit one or the other, and do the other for a semester. ... I didn't have any money. My salary had been very low, and I hadn't ever saved; not a nickel." Taking out loans and borrowing from friends, Jennie concentrated on becoming the first person in her extended family to graduate from college.

She was working hard to get her education, and was also struggling through a very difficult relationship at the same time. Virginia, her lover, owned an apartment building, and Jennie would help her fix up vacant units in return for her share of their living expenses. But Virginia had a serious drinking problem. Jennie found herself joining her all too often. "We lived together for five years, and it was just constant drinking, drinking, drinking." The relationship grew more and more volatile, and Jennie's studies suffered. Finally, she couldn't take it any more and decided she needed to leave.

A few months later, Jenny found herself going back out to the bars, and it wasn't long before another woman caught her attention. Cherie had come into the bar with her boyfriend, but he was quickly forgotten as Jenny and Cherie fell for each other and began a five-year relationship.

I was sitting next to her, and we went to the bathroom at the same time and realized, at that moment, that we were connecting. She tore a little heart out of toilet paper. She was the most exciting person I have ever known in my life. She was kind and loving. And she was Mormon. What I now know, looking back on it … I know what she was doing. It's okay that she did this for herself. She was trying to try out a new lifestyle, so to speak, to see if she was being suffocated by the Mormons, by her family, and all that stuff. And so, I was the first one on this list, which was a wonderful thing.

Cherie

Cherie took a job several years later that required her to move, and their relationship came to an end. "I'll never forget the day she told me she was moving, or the day she did move. One of the saddest moments of my life."

Jennie's teaching career began at 35. Student teaching made it clear to her that she preferred the challenge of teaching math, her minor, instead of French. After a short-term job or two, Jennie taught math at the same high school for 23 years.

Every summer I traveled someplace. One time, in 1977 in fact, I took that school year (1977-1978) off on a sabbatical, and I had a mini-motor home, a tiny thing, and drove all over the country. Traveled for 3½ months, and didn't come home during that time. I drove through 40 states. Saw every one of the outstanding things each of those states had to offer.

Frequenting the bars played a big role in her life in California, and it only slowed down once Jennie was teaching. For many lesbians, bars offered something other venues did not.

There were eight women's bars within easy walking distance of each other. And the routine was you started wherever you wanted to start, and made the rounds. If you only had one drink in each one, it's a lot! ... I'd take the bus home [from work], get out of my girl clothes, get into my boy clothes, and get in my car and hurry back to North Beach to make the bar scene. Next morning, wake up so hung over. Every night. Every work night, and every weekend. Weekends were brunches.

I do not know how I survived years of living like that. I really don't know how I survived not getting hurt, not getting thrown in jail or something.

That was the place to meet people. It was a place to be yourself. There wasn't much else you could do.

In spite of all the girlfriends and so much time in lesbian bars, Jennie was never out at her jobs. Selective friends knew, but no one else. "When they give an estimate as to the number of gay people there are in this country, I think they don't know the half of it. You only know the ones that don't mind if you know."

When it's appropriate, Jennie calls herself a gay woman.

That "lesbian" word was a dirty word. Well, not a dirty word, but people just didn't use that word as I was growing up. And I've never gotten used to it. I think of myself as gay. I don't think of "gay" as a noun. I am gay.

I was far more on the butch end of the scale when I still lived [in Houston], because that's how everybody was. From the day I first put on my brother's clothes, that's what I wanted to be. The older I get, the less sense that makes. Be yourself, and be whatever you are. You can be feminine one day, one minute, and something else the next.

Many of Jennie's friends from the bars were gay men, and when the AIDS epidemic hit in the early 80s her friends were not spared. "We formed kind of an unofficial organization. We named it the Marin AIDS Support Network. We raised all kinds of money, tons of money, to help these guys." She and her friends also acted as caretakers when they could, and helped in any way possible.

Sadly, most of her male friends died. Between the fear of AIDS, and a growing crackdown on driving under the influence, many of the bars went out of business.

It became apparent that the cost of continuing to live in California after retirement was too much, so Jennie returned to Houston, where she had grown up, starting over once again. She worried about having to make new friends, knowing most of the people she knew from 40 years earlier weren't likely to be around.

Instead of being lonely, she found herself busier than ever. Jennie built a large social network by joining LOAF [Lesbians Over Age Fifty], and donating time to AssistHers (a Houston organization that provides non-medical, in-home support and care to lesbians) and other service organizations. "There's just tons of people all over the place. Sometimes I have to say, 'No, I can't. I am too busy.' And it's good."

Golf is a passion of Jennie's. It used to be bowling, but back problems caused her to switch to golf. "Everybody has to have a pleasant thing to do in life." She's played for years, and even attended the Dinah Shore Tournament a dozen times. "It's fun. Just like a kid, I got so many autographs on so many hats and caps, including Dinah's, more than once."

Jennie never became fully comfortable about being a lesbian. While giving her interview at 73 years of age, she stumbled over saying the word "gay" as she spoke about bowling and golf. "Inevitably, if you're involved in a sport, you're going to meet some… some gay people. See, I have a hard time even saying that."

Jennie's mother moved into a retirement community where, just two streets over, two women lived together. The first year Jennie visited, her mother told her about her neighbors.

"It is so nice. They're cousins, you know. They live together, and it's so nice for both of them to have someone to be with." The next year I'm back again, and she said, "Remember, I told you about those two women who lived together over there? They're really not cousins. They're just friends."… The next year, my mother said to me, "You know those two women that I've been talking to you about? Well, some of the neighbors are saying

that they're queer. And I told them just because a woman lives with women all her life, that doesn't mean that she's queer." I'm thinking, "God, Mother. You are really blind." She's talking about me and she doesn't even know it.

Jennie's mother had had that fight with her over *The Well of Loneliness,* and had intercepted high school love notes, so she knew. "Just didn't want to admit she knew."

Jennie still remains cautious about letting anyone outside of her immediate friends know she is gay. "After my experiences in high school, I was never ever again going to put myself in that position — to be totally rejected by somebody I thought was important to me." Jenny had a cousin who was out to everyone. "Her attitude was 'take me or leave me, I don't care.' I always wished I could be that way, but I'm not."

It's never been openly discussed in the rest of her family either, but Jennie is sure they have to know. "How can they miss the way I live my life, the way I always dress." One time, an older male relative asked her, "Jennie, where do you find all these good-looking women?" to which she answered, "At the good-looking women store."

Jennie is currently living in Texas.
Interviewer: Arden Eversmeyer

Lois
Heindselman

Born April 1936 in Oklahoma
Interviewed in 2006 at age 70

Please release me, let me go.

When I was five years old, I remember my aunt came out from Oklahoma to visit us. I couldn't take my eyes off of her. I mean, I thought she was the prettiest thing I ever saw in my life.

That was Lois Heindselman's first hint of things to come. Of course, it took a few more years for her to understand what that attraction meant. Growing up in Tacoma, Washington, after the locusts drove her family out of Dust Bowl-wracked Oklahoma, Lois remembers going to the movies with her girlfriends.

We always saw every movie four or five or how many times. And these girls are sitting there saying, "Oh, I wish I could kiss Gordon MacRae." And I'm sitting there going, "Oh, I wish I could kiss Doris Day." And what do you say? I can't tell them this. I mean, you know it's not what you're supposed to be.

So, at a very early age, without even knowing the concept of being "in the closet," Lois knew she had to hide her feelings from everyone. "You can't go running around and telling people things like this … you don't even know what it means yourself."

The feelings continued, and as a high school sophomore she fell in love.

> *I would tell her I loved her, and she'd tell me she loved me. We'd pass notes back and forth, and all this stuff. And she said "Can I have your hand?"… She taught me this. She went squeeze, squeeze, squeeze. You know what that means? I love you. And then the other person goes squeeze, squeeze. "How much?" I was fifteen years old, and you know you can call it puppy love, but I'll tell you what, I could have cut off my arm for her. I mean, I plain flat loved her.… The only thing we really did was kiss a few times. That was all we ever did.*

Of course, the girl turned out to be straight, and Lois felt her heart had been broken.

Lois, like everyone else she knew, began dating boys. "I dated guys all over the place. Then I just got engaged to this fellow.… I thought, 'Well, everybody's got to do it some day.' Because in those days, if you were not married by the time you're 20, 21, 22 … people looked at you strange." He was a good enough guy, but Lois never felt she loved him.

Not yet 21, Lois and her friends (including her fiance) would sneak into a local bar to dance, and listen to the music. One night, the entertainment was an all-girl band. Lois found herself drawn to all the women, but a woman named Toby really caught her eye. Toby played bass violin, and she'd wander past their table during breaks, stopping to chat. Finally, she asked Lois to join her for coffee sometime.

> *For over a month or two, we just visited and talked about things. And she, in a nice gentle way, she introduced me … I thought there was not another soul in the world like me. I thought I was the only one that had these feelings.*

The band was about to move on, after playing at the same local club for three years, and Lois had returned the engagement ring to her boyfriend. Toby said, "You're mine now," and pled with Lois to leave for Florida with the band.

Well, what am I supposed to tell my mom and dad? How do I just say, "Mommy, Daddy, guess what? I'm going to run off with these girls here. I'm going to quit my job and go across the United States."

Lois was now 21, and knew her parents couldn't stop her, but she worried anyway. Finally she came up with an idea. She brought her parents to see the band perform, and convinced them that, if she traveled with them, she could learn to play an instrument and eventually join the band.

They left for Florida, and Toby began teaching Lois the basics of drumming. Within six months, they had moved to New Jersey. The original group had broken up. Toby and Lois took day gigs, while they worked to form a new band and line up some jobs. Cracks began to develop in their relationship as Toby, who was more than a decade older than Lois, began staying out late.

Lois wasn't sure what was happening between her and Toby. "It was hard for me. I got to thinking, 'This is not what love is supposed to be like — not in my book anyway.'"

Lois and Toby

The situation became even more confusing when another woman, 14 years her senior, began flirting with Lois. That was the first time Lois thought about leaving Toby.

So then it tempts you to go do something you shouldn't be doing. I never ever went to bed with her, but we'd kiss. … She wanted me to leave Toby. … But she had her own agenda too.

Toby and Lois practiced for about six months, put an ad in a musician's magazine looking for people to fill out a band, and hired a new member. Lois' first professional job was in Bay City, Michigan, in November 1958. The band went on to play all over the upper Midwest. At one gig, while they were setting up, the club owner walked over and told them that the dancer was ready to practice with them. Much to Lois' chagrin, the "dancer" turned out to be a stripper.

> You know when people ask you what is the most embarrass-ing thing in your life? I got to stand up for this one. ... Here we are in the middle of the afternoon just doing a run-through. Everybody had their clothes on, you know. I had never done such a thing like that in my life before. And I don't know what I'm doing. I'm not that much of a drummer in the first place. And Toby is just, "Watch. You got to watch her and catch her bumps. And whenever she ... you got to catch it with a rim-shot." ... I felt like a fool. I don't know what to do ... [The stripper] picked up that I'm this naive little baby, and she thought she was going to have some fun with me. We walked through this and ... I can't even watch her with her clothes on.
>
> So here comes this night ... and here was this house full of men. There's not one woman in the whole place. ... Well, here she comes out, and of course, by now, she's in her costume. And she told me already in the rehearsal, she said, "Now honey, you'll never miss one of my bumps because I always televise. I televise my bump, you know."

Playing with Lois, the woman went into her big windup, and did her first bump. Lois was so flustered, she missed the rim shot. The stripper stopped and turned to Lois. "Oh, you hurt me, Baby!" "Everybody just roared and roared. I must have turned every color that anybody could turn."

Lois realized, looking back, that she may have felt flustered by the stripper because she really did want to watch. As she gained more experience, both with the drums and with strippers, Lois played dozens of new venues all over the country, including an interesting two week booking in Alaska.

Arriving at the airport in Fairbanks, they were met by the club owner. And what was the first thing he wanted to know? "Youse girls going to do tricks for me?" When they politely declined, he said that was okay, but if they were interested they could make lots of money. He actually turned out to be a nice guy, and turned into their protector as their two week stay stretched out to six months.

Lois had gotten used to what she had to put up with as a part

Lois (upper right) and Toby (below her) with band mates.

of the job. Performers were expected to mingle with the customers during the intermissions, and they were expected to accept drinks.

We couldn't possibly drink it. I mean, nobody could drink all this… so what we'd do is order straight shots. And we had fruit jars. Every night we'd just pour the shots into fruit jars, and we'd take it home. Then once a month we'd throw a big party and invite everybody we knew!

As they continued to perform, the relationship between Lois and Toby continued to erode. During one month-long gig, Lois sang lead. "Every night I'd sing this song. It was 'Please Release Me, Let Me Go.' And I meant every single word I was singing in that song. I just prayed that I could get out of there." But that didn't happen.

Lois and her group soon became regulars on the USO tours. Traveling back and forth to different areas for two and three months at a time, the band went all over Europe, the Mediterranean, the Middle East, Hawaii, and even Point Barrow, Alaska. One of the last tours they made was the Far East, including stops in Vietnam during the height of the war. Since they were in a military zone, they were all issued papers saying they were captains, just in case they were captured. That way they would be treated as officers.

It was a hard and dangerous life, and nerves were frayed when a building they had just left was blown to smithereens. On another occasion, the band was awakened during the night.

They said to get your clothes on and don't turn on any lights. They put us all in little jeeps to take us out to the airfield, which wasn't that far away. … They didn't have any lights on either, and everything was totally black. The Vietcong were coming in, and they wanted to get us out of there so we wouldn't be right in the middle of this war thing. So they got us on this plane, and the plane takes off with no lights on. No runway lights. No nothing. Just taking off down there. And as we're going down the field, they're strafing us. … Thank god, they didn't hit us, and we got out of there.

They stopped touring with the USO soon after that. Lois and Toby returned to Tacoma, where they decided they'd take a correspondence course on tuning pianos. "Toby lasted about a week... but I kept up and finished it." Once she received her "diploma" in the mail, Lois realized that it was really worthless, and wondered how she ever thought piano tuning was something you can learn long distance.

Toby was insistent, and they went back on the road again. Lois soon found herself performing in Minneapolis on New Year's Eve. Their relationship just kept getting worse, as far as Lois was concerned, and she finally convinced Toby to let her go; at least she thought she had.

Toby called her a short time later. She told Lois she was dying and needed her to come help. "I'll come home and take care of you as long as you know that's where it is, that's what it is. We're not getting back together. We will not be together."

When Lois walked back into their old home in Tacoma where Toby was living, she greeted her with "I've got three piano students for you." Lois couldn't even play the piano, but she was, once again, drawn back in. "It was her way of keeping me there, roping me in."

Lois insisted that if she was going to teach piano lessons, she'd better learn to play. So she began her own lessons with Barbara, another woman in their musical community.

"I knew that somehow, somewhere in me, I was getting attracted and drawn to Barb. And she always pretended like she never looked at me. But it was not true. She did." Toby and Lois were living as roommates, but Toby went out of her way to give a different impression.

Decorating for Christmas that year, Lois got up her courage

Age 50 with Barbara

and pulled Barb under the mistletoe and "planted a smacker on her. And that was it. That was the end of the story.... When she touched me it was like I'd never been touched before in my life."

Lois knew what she wanted now, and there was no going back. She told Toby she was leaving, moving in with Barb. The response was, "WRONG."

When I came home to pack my things, she was sitting there with a fifth of Canadian Club and a gun. I'm carrying stuff out to the car and getting loaded up, and she said, "Lois, if you walk out that door, it's the last door you're going to walk out of." And I looked at her and I thought, "I've been two years with [you] and then ten years getting away, and I am not, I am not going back to the life I had before. I'd rather be dead." I said, "Toby, if

Showing off her drum skills at age 60

that's what you have to do, get used to it, because I'm leaving." And I just turned round, and turned my back to her, and walked out the door.

She succeeded in leaving that day, but Toby was persistent and made several more attempts to get her to come back; but Lois held her ground.

I'm so thankful every day. For a lot of years, Toby and I weren't that good of friends. But, of course, we ended up being truly, truly, dear wonderful friends. I love Toby with my heart and soul. It's not "in love," its love.

Living with Barbara came with its conditions. Children had never been a part of Lois' life before, but her new life included two teenagers and two cats (a tough one for Lois, a life-long dog-lover).

Barbara's piano needed tuning. Still fascinated with the process, Lois couldn't help but watch over the tuner's shoulder, and ask a barrage of questions. "Before Don left, he ended up making me a proposition, in a nice way, of course." Presented with the opportunity to be his apprentice and learn the craft, Lois began spending time in his workshop, and was faced with another dilemma. "What you need is a good man and about four or five kids," Don offered.

Knowing she couldn't sign on for months of working with him if she had to listen to comments like that, Lois decided to explain outright. "I got to tell you something before we sign this agreement. I'm gay and I don't mess around. ... If you can handle that, fine. If you can't, we'll just stop it right now." Other than saying he thought Lois was "barking up the wrong tree," Don was okay with Lois' boundaries, and taught her what she needed to know about tuning.

"I found my niche, after all these years. I was 31 years old and ... it was just a wonderful feeling." Entering a traditionally male profession, Lois was for decades the only woman piano technician in the Pacific Northwest. That in itself presented some difficulties, but it didn't take long for Lois to earn respect and a strong following. It was the start of a 35 year career in the field.

Lois lost Barbara to cancer after 25 years, and she found herself rambling around the house alone. She took ballroom dancing lessons, something she'd always wanted to do.

She also decided to venture off on an all-woman cruise. It was an experience she'd never forget.

Rumba lessons at age 60

I don't know how some-body could live, be as old as I am, be gay my whole life and not know … I never even knew that there were these things going on. I never knew that there was a place for women to go, and Barbara and I never heard of such a thing. … It was the first time in my life I felt what it was like to be normal. You know what I mean? I feel like everybody else gets to feel every day in their life. And I've never really felt that, because you always feel like something is wrong. If they even knew and realized the difference in how we have to feel because we happen to be this way, they'd do some second thoughts on it. You know, too many of them still believe and think that we … that it's our option, our choice.

Well, I got news.

Lois Heindselman died in 2009
Interviewer: Gloria Stancich

Beverly Hickok

Born October 1919 in California
Interviewed in 2003 at age 84

You are who you are.

Everything changed when I turned thirteen. I developed a huge crush on my teacher, which is par for the course. ... [She] was sort of like my mother, who was warm and funny. And she knew I had a crush on her.

Beverly recognized it was really just a crush, but it came at a critical time in her development.

The atmosphere at school changed, and then all my girlfriends became interested in boys. And I had no interest, at all. My best friend, Sue, now we are in high school. ... And she found a boyfriend. ... We had been inseparable; now she had a boyfriend and I was left out.

I had a terrible case of acne, which didn't help anything. My grades were good. But I was losing touch with the friends that I had in grammar school. And Sue not only had a boyfriend, but she was invited to join the girls' sorority at Alameda High, The Dianas. I wasn't. . . . I felt angry and became a loner.

Age 10

Beverly didn't really understand her feelings yet—she just knew she did not want to be with boys. This was in the 1930s. "I always had crushes on teachers and other girls. There was nothing written, no organizations, no books. I had no idea that there was such as thing as a lesbian."

Her parents were concerned, even though Beverly continuing to do well academically in school.

My parents became worried about me because all I wanted to do was stay home and read and go to the movies with my mother. And so they thought maybe a change of schools would help, that maybe I'd make new friends. They enrolled me in a private school here in Berkeley for my senior year in school.

The new school was a better fit, but Beverly's confusion didn't ease. She graduated from high school, and went on to college at the University of California, Berkeley.

It was my dad's idea that I join a sorority. I was surprised when I got a bid from the Tri Delts. I did not fit into this sorority at all. They were all into boys.

All the way through college I was planning on being a teacher, because in those days, there were not many alternatives for women. You could be a nurse, or a secretary, or a social worker. So, okay, teacher sounds good. A long vacation in summer appealed to me . . . so I went along with it.

Bored with her education classes, Bev suddenly found herself confronted with those confusing feelings again.

*In my senior year, I had a dream about my English professor.
I went up to her [in the dream] and leaned over the desk and
said, "I think you should know that I am sexually attracted
to you." It was only a dream, but it shattered me and changed
my life. I believed it when I woke up ... "My god! This is true."
I don't know of anyone else who discovered that they were gay
through a dream.*

Beverly knew she had to find some community. A friend
told her that she wouldn't believe it, but there was actually a bar
for gay women in San Francisco called Mona's. "I think she said,
'For gay women.' We didn't use the term 'lesbians' in those days.
She said they were even dancing together." Beverly had not told
her friend that she thought she was a lesbian, so she was surprised
when the San Francisco bar came up in conversation. "The timing
was such that I thought this is meant to be." The friend offered
to take Beverly and her roommate with her, so they could see for
themselves.

*My roommate said, "No." She was going to be a social worker
and I was going to be a teacher. So, I said, "Maybe it's something we should know about in our careers." ... We went with
this other girl. Of course, my roommate was interested but
appalled. I was completely fascinated.*

*A couple of weeks later, I told my roommate that I wanted
to go back. And she said, "You are kidding. That's ridiculous."
She wouldn't go with me. I went by myself, which took courage.
I just sat, you know; had big eyes, and had my drink and
looked, and didn't speak to anyone. I was too scared. Finally, I
went back another time; found a gay couple who told me some
of the key words.*

*At that same time, my grades were slipping since I was
confused about what was happening with me. I was beginning
to be worried about practice teaching coming up and my whole
choice of career. I knew I didn't have the right personality for it.*

Beverly had heard a woman give a presentation about sexual
deviation, and started into therapy with her. She was a therapist

working on her Ph.D. and was in the process of transferring to the University of California at Los Angeles. Beverly used her desire to continue the therapy to explain to her parents why she felt she needed to move to Los Angeles.

I did not think I could stay at home anymore. I had heard there was a place like Mona's in Los Angeles. So I thought, "If I transfer to UCLA to get my teacher's credentials, I will have a year to go to this other bar, which is called Tessie's, and find out if I really am gay." Of course, my parents were completely confused and upset, but they were paying for everything.

They agreed to let me go to UCLA, so I did. And I hated all my education classes. But I did go to Tessie's. ... Through my therapist, I met an older lesbian couple. They were in their thirties. They happened to live in an apartment quite close to Westwood, where I was renting. I became good friends, particularly with one of them; her name was Chris. Very warm person. ... Very interested in what I was going through. She was always there as a sounding board.

Then practice teaching came along and, as I had suspected, I was a complete failure. I would prepare, but have stage fright, and was not good at all.

Struggling with the experience she was having teaching, Beverly began a brief affair with a friend of Chris'. "She was glad to have sex with me but it didn't work out. I questioned, 'Am I really gay?' And I was thinking if I'm a teacher, I can't be gay." Beverly went to Chris for advice once again.

"You are who you are," she said. "Why don't you just give up the idea of teaching if you are going to be that unhappy?

31 years old

It looks as if you are heading for a nervous breakdown."

Beverly did receive her secondary teaching certificate but, taking her friend's advice, quit school, and took a job in a defense plant as a riveter.

"Rosie the Riveter" 1943

> *My parents were completely taken aback. Five years of college, and then I wound up as a riveter. But it worked out. I worked as a riveter, and I met an older woman. So I moved in with her. I think I was with her at least a year. I knew from the beginning it wouldn't last forever.*

It was a sexual relationship that Beverly enjoyed, but the woman had a drinking problem. It did, however, show Beverly that it was possible to live with another woman.

Beverly gave in and got a teaching job. Her parents repeatedly expressed their concern for her well-being. They pointed out that she couldn't just keep on drifting. Assigned to teach both social studies and physical education, Beverly once again felt out of place as a teacher.

> *I was a misfit. Somehow I lasted out the year. ... I knew I'd never teach again as long as I lived. This was 1944 by now.*
>
> *And so again, I escaped; this time by joining the WAVES in the Navy. And that was a good experience for me. I was stationed in Washington, D.C.*
>
> *You couldn't leave the base unless you had your uniform on; or you shouldn't. If you were caught, you'd be dead. Of course I had leaves, and I headed for New York. I was going to bars in Greenwich Village. I had a few adventures.*

After leaving the service, Beverly decided to give college another try. A cousin was going to library school in Berkeley. That sounded good to Bev. Even with the GI Bill footing part of the cost, unless she wanted to work part-time and take years to complete the program, Beverly found it necessary to live back at home again.

> *In one way, it was wonderful. My mother spoiled me rotten, as she always had. I didn't have to do anything around the house. But socially … socially I had nothing except going to school. I made casual friendships with some of the girls, but every once in a while I'd feel the urge to be with my own kind.*
>
> *I'd lie to my parents and say I was going out to the movies with one of my friends from school, and go into the city to Mona's. … In 1947, I lucked out and I met Cecil Davis. We were together for 41 years.*

Beverly and Cecil in 1950

With her degree in hand, Beverly started her library career in 1947, working in the document department at the university where she had gotten her degree.

At work in 1963

I didn't feel satisfied with it, so I went to the personnel department to see if there were any other openings, and there was one: a temporary position to select materials for a new institute that had just been created, The Institute of Transportation and Traffic Engineering. I didn't know anything about civil engineering. I quit my job and took it.

Beverly was authorized to select and purchase all the materials needed to build a library for this emerging field of study.

I was told to spend $10,000 in a month. I ordered books, journals, and reports, not knowing anything about the subject. And the director said, "Well, I think it should be catalogued and something done with it." So I was hired as the librarian. I stayed in that job for 32 years. When I left, it was one of the largest university transportation libraries in the United States.

My job was to do research for the professors, and compile bibliographies on certain subjects, organize the library, and help the students. Graduate students came from all over the world, and we had many, many foreign students. ... I enjoyed it. I was doing something worthwhile, and I was good at it.

In 1961, Beverly and Cecil together bought a house with a view of the Golden Gate Bridge. Cecil was a professional photographer, and for years they traveled.

But she developed Lupus. One of the side effects was facial lesions. She didn't want anyone to see her, so she became a recluse. For the last ten years, we didn't have any friends. Part of it was she was afraid I would leave her if we had friends over to the house.

I had retired in 1980, and I kept busy. I took writing classes. I took painting classes. No contact with lesbians. I had some friends that I had known at work that I had lunch with and went to the movies, but Cecil would get frantic.

Then Cecil died unexpectedly of a ruptured hernia, leaving Beverly even more aware of her isolation.

After living with someone for 41 years, it was quite difficult to adjust to being alone. I decided that I was still young enough to make some friends. I needed to find another partner, so I started looking. I got a copy of the San Francisco Bay Times, and they had something in there for older lesbians.

At first, Beverly connected with other women through two different local social groups, Retiring Women and Entertaining Women. She heard about a conference on the west coast that was intended specifically for old lesbians. Beverly joined the planning committee and made lots of new connections and friends. She also got involved in OLOC, when it formed a few years later.

When she heard that Golden Threads, a social organization for older lesbians, was holding an event in Provincetown, she and a friend decided to go together. Beverly enjoyed it, but didn't meet anyone that first time. Meanwhile, she started writing to a new connection, Doreen. She returned to PTown the next year, 1990.

"That's when I met Doreen. I was 70, and it was the beginning of a new life. And so, you know the end of the story!"

Bev continues to reside in California.
Interviewer: Bea Howard

Note from Beverly: My novel, *Against the Current; Coming Out in the 1940s,* is based very closely on my own life. (It is available through Amazon.com as well as many women's bookstores.) ISBN 1413435467

Marie
Mariano

Born June 1922 in Idaho
Interviewed in 1998 at age 76

This is where I belong.

The first thing I remember about anything is getting a doll for Christmas. I think I must have been about four. I remember piling the boxes up behind the fence to trade my doll to the next door neighbor for a gun and holster. My Daddy took me down and bought me overalls and a little shirt, and a gun and holster. Then I went from there.

Marie's grandparents had been political exiles from Italy, and she and her siblings were raised to be patriotic Americans. But the local atmosphere in Pocatella, Idaho didn't make that easy.

I don't think there was a boy in the first, second, or third grade that I didn't give a bloody nose to, because they called me a "wop" or a "dago." They talk about prejudices… prejudices were there, very much so. I don't know if many people remember that the veterans from World War I were not given anything, benefits or anything.

Marie's father had fought in World War I, and had spent years in and out of hospitals unable to work. So when he died just before the Depression, her family was left destitute. They lived with her grandparents. Her mother went back to finish nurse's training, and the children got odd jobs.

I felt very bad that I was not a boy. There were not any positions for girls. But I talked them into letting me have a paper route, and I delivered my papers on foot. I had a big paper route. I'd get up at 3 o'clock in the morning and deliver my papers, and I'd still get to school on time. ... I did make enough money to pay for shoes and things we needed.

I think the best thing that happened to us growing up in the Depression is in that section of the country, they have harvest season. They did not have vacation [from school] like they do here. ... At harvest vacation, if you did not own a farm, you had to farm out to some farmer. ... Claude and Noel and myself, we would sit on the steps of our house, and the farmer would pick us up between 3:30 and 4 a.m. We picked potatoes, onions, carrots [and apples, and berries] and cabbage. ...

Most of the kids would pick their pick for money. We did not. We picked for the supply. So, for every 300 pounds of whatever we picked, we got 100 pounds for ourselves. And, in two weeks time, between us ... we had all our supplies to eat.

Nursing was an incredibly demanding job, and it almost killed Marie's mother. The job truly wore her mother out, and Marie's grandmother stayed with them to help care for the family.

Nurses worked twelve to fifteen hours a day for $40 a month. I'd sit out on the porch when my mother was so ill, and people would come by and ask me, was I going to be a nurse like my mother? And I would say, "Hell, no! That's the last thing I want to be!"

I really did NOT want to be a nurse. No way, no how. I wanted to go to work on the railroad. In fact, there was a woman who lived three blocks down from me who, every morning, carried a lunch pail and wore her striped overalls.

I was going to work on the railroad like Mrs. Moore. I wasn't going to become no nurse!

Marie was lucky that her mother's family believed that it was important for the children to get an education, and they stayed in school. When their mother died, Marie gave up her dream of working on the railroad, and took charge. "I realized that I had to have an education, because I was in charge of my family."

Authorities tried hard to divide Marie and her siblings between relatives, but she wouldn't hear of it. "There was a guy by the name of Judge McDavids... I stood up and told him in the court I'd see us all dead before I'd see any of us with my father's folk. And I meant that."

If she wasn't in school, Marie was usually working. "I did finally win a bicycle, so that I could carry on my [paper] route and get a bigger route." She also peddled magazines such as *True Stories*, *True Romance* and *True Detective,* and her siblings took odd jobs to contribute. But sometimes, Marie just had to escape from it all.

I kept my father's Army stuff, and I packed his knapsack and I went to the mountains. I liked to be by myself. There's a mountain named Mount Kindport, and I was the first woman to climb it. I must have been around 16. I loved to go to the hills and be by myself.

Tomboy was a necessity for me, because the things I had to do women didn't do. I thought girls were sissies. In my neighborhood, I played with the boys. ... In school, I was an all-around athlete: I ran and I won the hundred-yard dash, I was in the band, I was in the drum and bugle corps, I played baseball, I played basketball, the 100-yard, 75-yard, 50-yard and pole vault. At one of the tournaments, I won first place for all of them. And the coach said to me, "God-damn, why can't you be a boy?!" I said, "Don't ask me. I wish to heck I was a boy!"

Marie's first serious crush on another girl came when she was a junior in high school.

Ann was my first. Ann to me was the lady. I know the way I started to treat her was like a boy [would]. I put her coat on for her, walked on her left, opened the door for her, treated her to all these things. ... Ann could've told me, "Jump in the lake" and I would've jumped.

Even though it had been a one-sided relationship, when Ann joined the Army and left, Marie was devastated. "I really thought I'd been abandoned. That was the biggest hurt I could remember as a young person. Ann going off and leaving me."

Marie finished high school at 17, and after waiting a year until she was old enough, even with all her strong feelings against it, she entered nurse's training. She went to the same school her mother had attended, and found that an added burden. "Some of the nuns wanted to be my mother, and by that time I didn't feel like I needed a mother. ... I was able to get home. I was able to see to the utilities. I was able to see to the groceries."

She didn't, however, go straight through nursing school. Students were required to live at the school, but Marie had to make sure things were okay at home, and she was constantly in trouble for sneaking away. Tired of it all, she quit.

I put on a pair of overalls, blue shirt, packed a lunch bag and went to work at the railroad in Pocatello, Idaho. I worked in the [railroad] roundhouse, and I loved it. I thought it was real great. I loved to come home with my greasy hands and use my Lava soap.

She didn't stay there long, though, since the war was on and people gave her a hard time. "I had a difficult time because of my mother ... My mother was like a shrine in the town. They just thought it was terrible that here I was, almost a nurse, and I was going to work at the railroad." After six weeks at the railroad, Marie came home one day to find two nuns at her house. "They had come to talk me into going back to nursing because, in reality, I only had six weeks, plus my study for state boards, to graduate." The nuns finally conceded there could be allowances for Marie to both stay in school and help at home with her family, so she did go back and finish.

Marie's family lived within a few miles of a reservation, and Native Americans played a big role in her early life.

The Indians were very fond of my mother, like everyone else. So we kids would go out to the reservation and we'd play. ... One of my first roughneck playmates, that I felt could play like I could, (could swim and hunt and climb and fish) was Lucille Pocatello, who was Chief Pocatello's daughter. She and I became very close friends.

Age 21, Nursing Graduation

So when I got out of nurse's training, I had gone and applied to go into the Army. In the meantime, I went out to the reservation because everybody had known my mother. They all knew us kids. I had two beautiful horses I could ride. I spoke Shoshone and Blackfeet. I really will say that my being able to survive—and I think even today you could drop me off any-where and I could survive—that's from what I learned from the American Indians.

Stationed at Fort Hall and working for Public Health, Marie and another woman delivered all the babies, gaining a set of skills that was about to come in handy. An urgent need arose for a nurse to work in Public Health in Alaska, and Marie was the closest nurse available.

At that time, they had a law that you had to be more than 25 to be allowed into Alaska, but they waived that to let me go while she [the regular nurse] had to take leave. ... So I went by dogsled from village to village to deliver Indian babies, Eskimo babies. ... If they would have allowed, I would have stayed. I loved Alaska.

I was only there six weeks, then I came back. By this time they'd closed the Fort Hall hospital because all the doctors were gone [to the war]. So I went to Schurz, Nevada, which is near Hawthorne.... Again, I had a horse. I had a beautiful Palomino.... I made rounds in Schurz, Nevada, on horseback. If I found somebody who was ill, I came back for my staff car.

Marie had to wear her Public Health uniform most of the time, but she much preferred the more casual dress riding a horse necessitated. "I was in nothing but boots and Levi's." During her time in Nevada, Marie learned to speak Paiute and Mayo, and earned herself the nickname of "The Blond-Headed Shoshone."

All the while Marie was working for Public Health, she was on call to the Army. Just before her 23rd birthday, she was called to active duty, and stationed at Madigan Army Medical Center in Washington. "Because I could handle a gun, I was out on the rifle range. I laughed and laughed because the WACS thought the Army nurses were just the biggest sissies." The WACS had been formed during WW II, but the Army Nurse Corps had been in existence since before WW I.

Marie spent time in Japan, Oklahoma, and Texas where she finally settled. She was determined she was never going back to Pocatello to live. She knew that if she did, she would end up taking care of her family once again.

Marie did spend some time back in Idaho, in the mountains she loved, when she had leave. A doctor she knew let her use his cabin in Sun Valley. As she prepared for one of her stays in the mountains, he asked her a big favor.

Dr. Dean says, "You know Ernest Hemingway?... He's up there, and he wants to go after a bighorn sheep.... He wants it for a trophy.... The man who was to be his guide didn't show up. Will you do me a favor? Take him up into the Sawtooths, and be his guide."

Marie hated the idea of shooting a bighorn, especially just for a trophy, but she felt she owed the doctor asking the favor for letting her use his cabin. Marie met with Hemingway the next day, and helped him select the right gun from his vast collection. Then, without any remorse, she promptly led him in the wrong direction!

When she was stationed in Texas, Marie befriended a young Native American woman, who was also serving in the area. They both liked working on cars. They bought an old beater, and spent lots of time chasing around, having a good time. After awhile, her friend disappeared for a few days. When the woman came back, Marie was shocked by her friend's appearance. She thought maybe the woman had been hospitalized, and asked what happened.

"I've been through three days of torture.... Someone said I am homosexual. I've been grilled worse than anybody could've been grilled by the FBI. They kept me under lights. They questioned me. They threatened me. I'll never live through what they've done to me." I'll never understand why they took her and they didn't take me. We chased around together. I'll never know. But she got orders, and I never did hear from her again. I don't know whether they ousted her or what they did.

Marie reconnected with a close friend, Kathy, when she took a new assignment. "The thing between Kathy and I ... friends, buddies, a bond that never can be broken." When Marie's grandmother's health was failing, they drove together to Pocatello, shut up the house, and brought her grandmother back to stay with them in Texas. It wasn't long before her grandmother died, and her wish had been to be

Headed to Japan in 1945

cremated. The only crematory in the area was miles away, so Kathy rode with Marie and her grandmother's body to Dallas, and gave up her holiday.

> *We lived off the post at Fort Hood. There was a whole group of us that lived off the post. ... Nobody talked about it. You were buddies and friends that chased around together. ... Jean and Bennie were the first ones to get a TV. We'd have dinners; we'd go fishing together. It would be no different if my neighbor and her husband was coming over. There was nothing that nobody could say. There was no holding hands, there was no mush or goo, there was nothing. ... So we were a group that chased around together. Nothing was ever said.*
>
> *This is when I knew. I said, "Yeah, I belong. This is where I belong."*

Kathy (on the left) with Marie in 1946

Marie finally realized she was a lesbian, and that she loved Kathy, but their relationship was never sexual.

Sarah, another of the women in Marie and Kathy's group of friends, began to catch Marie's attention. Their relationship slowly grew, and eventually they became a committed couple.

Marie had been stationed in the region when the bomb was dropped on Nagasaki. She also did a horrific tour in a MASH unit during the Korean conflict. Specializing in care of prisoners with psychiatric problems was extremely taxing. Marie felt that many of the prisoners were badly mistreated. An incident pushed her so far she even went AWOL. The Army would bring in new nurses that outranked her, but had much less experience, and she'd be forced to do things their way. A particularly sadistic nurse, who was a "damn Yankee," got to her. Marie requested a transfer.

"If you don't transfer me, you're going to be burying one nurse and court-martialing another for murder!" I just knew if I had to see her make a boy with a 104° temperature stand at attention, or remake his bed because it didn't suit her, that I was going to beat the living shit out of her right then and there.

The transfer was denied, and Marie simply took off her uniform, put on her cowboy boots and Western shirt, and took off. She returned ten days later, fully expecting to face a court martial for being AWOL. "I figured it was better than killing the woman." Surprisingly, when she returned, the chief nurse called her in and took the blame for not having adequately supervised the sadistic nurse.

Whenever possible, Marie went back to school where she was stationed, but she was frustrated when credits she earned in one location were not accepted at the next. After an especially emotionally draining post in a burn unit, Marie left the military, and began working at a civilian hospital. Kathy left the service too, and she took a job at the VA, where her time in the Army would count toward retirement. Marie also considered that, but wanted to work where her schedule would allow her to go to school.

Marie managed to earn a B.A., a B.S., and a M.S. degree while studying around her nursing shifts at Methodist Hospital in Houston, and decided to leave nursing to teach. "I resigned my job at Methodist. I just went ahead, and went to see what it would be like to teach. I loved it. I taught literature, I taught Russian literature and English, and I truly loved the University." Marie grew unhappy as her students in the '60s became more cavalier about their education. She'd been accustomed to the strict discipline of both the Catholic schools she'd attended, and of the Army.

Marie returned to nursing when Methodist Hospital agreed to let her set up a Neuro-Nurse Specialist course. But this time, she returned as a nursing instructor. It wasn't until she'd been at Methodist 36 years that she retired.

I've thought of this many times. When I sat on the steps [as a teenager] and people would ask me was I going to be a nurse like my mother, and I'd say, "Hell, no. That's the last thing I'm going to be!" It WAS the last thing I was!

Throughout all Marie's time in Japan, Korea, and elsewhere, Sarah had always been there for her. In 1984, Sarah had a heart attack, and when the surgeons tried to clean out her carotid artery, she had a massive stroke.

She was sick and really almost incapacitated for about five years before she became completely bedfast … she was more mentally alert than I was, because I was too tired to be mentally alert. The thing that bothered me the most with Sarah is the fact that she wanted to die to relieve me of the responsibility.

Marie and Sarah had never acknowledged their relationship to anyone, even amongst their friends, other women couples. It simply wasn't discussed. This made it even harder when Sarah died.

Sarah, Marie's partner of 29 years

For fifteen years after Sarah was gone, Marie found herself bonding with her straight friends. Her true self began to emerge again, and she started working at the hospice caring for gay men dying of AIDS. But she still didn't come out to anyone.

Then one day when she happened to be volunteering at the hospice, her attention was caught by two women sitting together; one was obviously sick.

I sat down between the two women, and I told 'em about Sarah, and I told 'em I knew how they felt. I told 'em, I said, "You know, once in a lifetime comes around someone who loves you better than anyone else." But, I said, "Life has to go on. The thing you have to do is remember the happy things. Remember the happy, crazy things you did. Remember the fun you had."

American Legion Commander, 1986

The women asked Marie if she knew about LOAF, a local social organization for older lesbians. "You know, to be a person 77 years old and to have led such a sheltered life, it wasn't because I was afraid really." Between family obligations, school, work and taking care of Sarah, she'd just never felt a need to seek out a wider group of lesbians.

LOAF [Lesbians Over Age Fifty] opened a whole new world to Marie. "When I went to LOAF, these were people who understood where I came from, and where I had been." When somebody asked Marie if she'd come so she could find a new companion, she quickly set them straight.

> *That was the furthest thing from my mind. I went there to talk to people who would understand and know what I had been through: people who I could talk to about Sarah and our life together, the crazy things we did, the crazy things we didn't do, the problems we had, the problems we didn't have.*

At 77 years of age, Marie finally found her community and her voice, and she came out. If she'd known earlier in her life about the gay community, bars, and bookstores, her life might have been different. At the very least, she might have been better prepared to deal with the two unsettling encounters that took place when she was a teenager.

The first happened when she was sent to a workshop while in nurse's training and, to save money, had to share a bed with another student.

> *I turned over to go to sleep, and Ripley is playing around with me. And all the time, she's saying, "Oh, now, come on Marie." And she used profanity with me. And she was going, "Don't give me that noise. Who in the blank do you think you're kidding?" And I truly did not know what the heck she was talking about. And she says, "Oh, hell. I give up with you. You're just not going to admit anything to anybody."*

Marie was truly confused. Not too much later, shortly before she joined the Army, Marie escorted her high-school crush, Ann, on a trip to San Francisco. While Ann went to meet with her father, Marie wandered around town.

> *I wore a good-lookin' Western shirt, I had cowboy boots, I had a good lookin' pair of Western pants on, and my wide Western belt. And I thought, "Boy, I'm a good lookin' Westerner!" And this is the part of me, too, that says I'm going like a boy. That inner part of me was there.*

Marie had heard the term "gay bar" but didn't really know what that meant. And back in Idaho, it wasn't unheard of for people to safely wander into bars, have a drink and listen to the piano player.

> *So I went into this bar ... and I'm sitting there drinking and along comes this... I guess what they call today a "diesel dyke." Anyway, she sat down and talked to me. And I'm a friendly person and I talk to everybody.*

After they had been at the bar for awhile, Marie agreed to go to the woman's apartment nearby so they could relax.

She says, "Make yourself comfortable." Well, I'm comfortable in my boots and things. ... So I'm sitting there at the table and then she puts her arm around me ... and next thing you know, she picks me up! I didn't weigh any more than about 120 pounds. ... She grabs my shirt and says a whole bunch of things to me that I didn't even know what she was talking about. And she says to me, "Don't give me that old crap! Don't sit here and tell me you don't know what I'm about."

I never thought anything about the fact that she was going to take me to bed. I just thought she was going to kill me. Because I hadn't been taken to bed by anybody. ... I fought. I really fought. I don't know how I got away from her, but she lifted my shirt. She couldn't get to my pants ... because I wore a real heavy belt. But she pulled my hair, she hit me. Man, she really hit me hard.

Here I am 19, and not even knowing what was happening to me.

Marie managed to get away, badly shaken and bruised.

She knows her life, and instances like these, would have made much more sense if she'd had access to the books and friends she found when she came out in her late 70s. She still marvels at her good fortune, as she tries to understand what made her stop to talk to those two women at the hospice, when she could have just gone home.

"Events happen when they are meant to."

Marie died in 2008.
Interviewer: Arden Eversmeyer

Vera
Martin

Born June 1923 in Mississippi
Interviewed in 2000 at age 77

We are a project in progress.

Natchez, Mississippi, was an extremely difficult place for a child like Vera. She was born there to a mother of African-American heritage who, soon after giving birth to Vera, made it clear "she absolutely did not want a baby, and that she absolutely was not taking care of her." Six-months pregnant, Vera's mother had married a man who was not the baby's father. When Vera was born three months later, her step-father contacted relatives and said, "If you want the baby to survive, you'd best hurry and come and get her."

The people who became Vera's guardians weren't blood relatives, but they had been her mother's guardians as well. Thus her life began, growing up totally isolated on a farm in Louisiana, with substitute parents who were already in their late fifties and early sixties when they took Vera in.

Vera adored her foster father. "When he put his foot out of

the track, my foot went right in it. I followed him everywhere, as often as I could."

Her relationship with her foster mother was another story. "I went into a total panic when [my foster father] left home because she was so mean. And I knew, in his absence, I was gonna get it for whatever reason she could come up with."

When Vera was five, she was sent to visit her biological mother, and her mother's husband, in Dallas.

> I really looked forward to his [her mother's husband] coming home nights, because he was really and truly a very, very kind man. And she was a mean human being. I remember her saying to me, almost a daily thing, "I don't know why in the hell I ever let them bring you here! I'll be so glad when Daddy [her guardian] comes and gets you."

Vera had arrived in May and had to wait until the Christmas holiday, seven miserable months, before she could leave. While there, she did attend a school. "I couldn't print, but I could write." Vera had learned to write by filling out catalog orders for her illiterate foster mother. "I copied this whole story out of a book in the classroom, and brought it home and showed it to [my mother]; she slapped me on the head with it, and said, 'That's a lie. You didn't write this.'" Vera couldn't wait to go back to Louisiana, and only saw her biological mother twice more before she was sixteen.

Living with her guardians in the summer, Vera was passed off to her foster mother's mother in a nearby town during the school year. "We're talking about a lady who was nine years old when the slaves were freed." When Vera was thirteen, this woman became ill and moved to the farm with her daughter. "That was the end of [formal] school for me." She was home schooled for the next few years, yet managed enough credits to graduate from high school.

Major changes came to Vera's life when she was sixteen. Her biological mother was living in California with a new husband. He insisted she bring Vera out to live with them so she could have a better life and get an education. It took quite a bit of maneuvering to make it happen, but in the end her foster father drove Vera to where she could catch a Greyhound bus, and sent her on to Dallas.

When she got there, she stayed with a distant relative before the next leg of the trip.

> *The way they arranged for me to get from there to Los Angeles was that people put ads in the paper. They were going from Point A to Point B, and they wanted somebody who wanted to share the ride and share expenses. ... Well, the person they hooked me up with was a white male, who picked up another white male.*
>
> *From Dallas to someplace in Phoenix, Arizona, I was in this car with the two white males. ... The driver of the car was a decent person. The passenger was determined that he was going to molest me. I was absolutely scared to death. Add that we were crossing the states of Texas, New Mexico, and Arizona, and I wasn't supposed to go into any restaurant. ... When I got to New Mexico, I was sick of that. I got out of the car and went into this steak house, and sat down and ordered a meal. And I enjoyed it, but all the customers, I'm sure, left with indigestion!*

Vera was relieved when they finally made it to Los Angeles, and she was dropped off where her mother was living. She took an immediate dislike to her mother's new husband. From her perspective, the new situation wasn't any better than what she had left.

Even though Vera had already graduated from high school, her mother insisted on enrolling her in a nearby junior high, and lied about her age. Vera was understandably bored by having to sit through classes of materials she already knew, and by having to socialize with kids much younger than herself. She quickly moved on to the high school. Since she'd already taken most of the classes, high school took her just two years.

17 years old

Three months shy of graduating from high school a second time, eighteen year old Vera ran off, and secretly married her boyfriend. When her mother found out, she was livid. Her mother then lied to all her friends, saying that Vera had gotten married because she was pregnant. It wasn't true, but Vera did have a baby after 11 months of marriage.

Marriage was a way to escape the dysfunctional life Vera had been living with her biological mother.

> I knew that sooner or later, if I stayed any longer, one of us was gonna get hurt, my mother or me. ... So I got married. And I liked everything about my own house. I was a compulsive neatnik. I was an excellent cook. I was a great manager. ... Any of the domestic stuff was just great.
>
> But I ran into a brick wall when I had to get involved in the intimate part of it. I can remember every time I was in this situation, I would end up getting up, going into the bathroom after the fact, and throwing up my guts. I just couldn't stand the smell of the semen. I just didn't like anything about it. But I didn't know why. I had no words for it. I had no explanation. There were no adjectives to describe what was going on with me. I didn't have a clue.
>
> As time goes by, I realize that I gravitated toward people who were known as queers. He [her husband] had a first cousin who was a lesbian. ... When I went to live with his grandfather, her friends came to his house all the time. I remember begging her, when they were going to go out, "Please let me go! Why can't I?!" And [the cousin] wouldn't, because she knew she'd get into a world of trouble with his family. And that was a clue. But I didn't know what to do with that information. I had no idea. I just knew I wanted to go. And I was not allowed.

Vera's daughter was born in 1943. "In those years, you stayed in the hospital for ten days when the baby was born. I left at the end of the ninth day, because [her husband] had gotten his induction papers, and was going to be leaving to go to the military." Even though she and her husband were living independently, renting a house for $25 a month, he and her mother came up with a scheme that resulted in Vera and her daughter moving back in with her mother. That situation was a complete disaster and didn't last long. Vera and her daughter left that home. She opted to share a house with two other young women until her husband returned from the service.

Life was good. Vera and her daughter, Roni, enjoyed each other's company, and spent time together going to concerts and Saturday matinees at the theater. Vera's activist side was growing, and, in addition to helping form a group that planned activities for children, she was involved in various civic and political organizations. "I was always out marching with a placard in my hand, some place about something. My mug shot was in all the police stations, and all the sheriff's stations, because I was a troublemaker."

Vera gave birth to her second child, a son, when her daughter was nine. Working hard to meet her family's needs, Vera pushed her underemployed husband to pull it together, and to get a better job. With Vera's help, he passed the required tests, got a job with Douglas Aircraft, and was quickly promoted.

> In order to take the supervisor position, he had to work swing shift. ... That's when everything started to unravel. He always had been a womanizer. I used to circumvent them [his involvements with other women] because as soon as I found out who the person was, I would invite her to the house for dinner. And then I would do things to provoke him, so he could show what he was really like.

Vera's innovative tactic worked for a long time, but eventually she'd had it. Coming home late, and practically ignoring her one too many times was the final straw.

> It was like lightning struck. I sprang into the bed, straddled him, and got him by the jugular. I was going to kill him. And all of a sudden, it was like someone pulled the switch. I realized what I was doing and I let go. He was so shocked, and so off guard, that he didn't know what to do to get rid of me. I could very easily have choked him to death.

Afraid to stay, afraid of what might happen, he fled. By eight o'clock the next morning, Vera had called the locksmith, and by nine o'clock the locks were changed.

A year later, they divorced. In spite of all the nasty things he had been saying about her, when it came to determining custody of their children, her husband, who didn't want the responsibility, told the judge Vera was a wonderful mother, and that he felt the children would be best off with her. Supporting herself and two children wasn't easy. Down to just 18¢, Vera finally found someone to watch the children, and she took on two extra jobs which, of course, took their toll on her health. Divorced and in her mid-thirties, Vera took another big step in her life.

I was going to a lot of wild parties, and I ran head on into this lesbian, and we had this thing. And I liked what went on. And I said to myself, "You didn't throw up!"... During marriage, I would hear other women bragging, and just having the jolliest old time talking about orgasms. "What? What's that?!" I didn't know what the hell an orgasm was. Well damn! I sure knew after that encounter!

Vera's first big love affair was with Kay, a woman from Japan. Like Vera, Kay had two children.

We just hit it off. ... I'd go a couple times a week for dinner, and on the weekend I'd take the kids, and we go over and hang out. ... Before you knew it, we were in a love affair. I was thirty-six when I met her. She was twenty-nine.

Once, after they'd had a tiff, Vera went to see Kay. She was sitting out on the stoop. "I stopped to talk to her. We talked about what had happened, and why it had happened. And we were both sorry." Vera invited Kay to her son's upcoming birthday party. As the event was about to begin, the phone rang. It was Kay's housekeeper, telling her that Kay had suddenly become ill the day before, had been taken to the hospital, but had died. After some investigation, Vera found out that the hospital had delayed treating Kay while they tracked down her husband and the insurance information. When they finally admitted her, it was too late, and Kay had hemorrhaged to death.

"It took me about three years to pull my act together. That was the first big love affair. Hit me like a ton of bricks … like a ton of bricks." But falling in love had cleared up many of her questions. "I knew that this was the problem for all those things I couldn't name and couldn't describe."

Vera's primary job, at this time, was working for Los Angeles County. She started out in a temporary position and took every exam offered, and applied for every open position she knew of, determined to get a better paying, permanent position. But it was an uphill battle. Men were given preferential treatment as they returned to the work place. To make things worse, Vera had a confrontation with a supervisor.

"She gave me this long speech about how she tried to be good to 'you people'. … I've always been a rebel, and, I mean to God, that was the operative word… 'You people.'" Challenging the woman, Vera demanded, "What the hell do you mean, 'you people'?" When the supervisor tried to cover up the situation by firing her, Vera went above the supervisor's head. The woman went on to try every trick she knew to keep Vera from getting a better job with the county. Vera was even written up by her supervisor for arranging a surgical procedure she needed without getting this woman's permission.

Sure that the personnel office was aware of the situation, and equally aware that she was not going to sit by quietly and take it, Vera did finally get the permanent position, and continued to work toward better and better job postings. She learned the ins and outs of thirteen different county departments, and it became clear she was an invaluable asset to the county. That's not to say she always played nice. Vera was deeply involved in the union, questioned unjust rules and regulations, and worked hard to improve conditions for all her co-workers whenever an opportunity arose.

Early in her career with the county, Vera was called to task for her refusal to sign a loyalty oath. She felt she had pledged her loyalty when they hired her. Back and forth it went until she received a registered letter summoning her to appear before the Chief Administrative Office for the County of Los Angeles.

He explained to me that he was not attempting to coerce me, but it was very important that I sign the document "for the preservation of my employment." I replied, "You are coercing me! You've broken my arm and you're beating me over the head with the bloody end of it!"

Vera went on to point out to them that they expected her to sign an affidavit stating she never belonged to a list of organizations, all of which served to protect the rights of minorities. The county seemed to be working on the assumption that the listed organizations (which included the Urban League and NAACP) were working to overthrow the government. Vera would not accept their premise, and let them know why.

It is blatantly obvious to me you don't have the White Citizens Council, nor the Ku Klux Klan, nor the Aryan Nations [on the list]. And I don't know of any three organizations that are more destined to overthrow the government than they are.

The county finally relented. They allowed Vera to sign an amended document, adamantly stating her support of progressive organizations, and lambasting the county for ignoring the threats of the like of the Klan. She didn't lose her job, but Vera was now labeled a communist.

With her daughter Roni grown, married, and a new mother, Vera's living situation changed. Feeling it was essential that Roni and her family have a place to live on their own, Vera opted to let them take her house, and she and her son Tony moved into an apartment and started from scratch again. In the process of getting some upholstery work done, Vera formed a friendship with Eddie.

[He] was really a breath of fresh air. I had dated a few other fellows, and they were like an octopus. They all had about nine or ten hands! I was exhausted at the end of the evening. They didn't seem to understand when I said "no," that's what I meant.

Eddie was different, and they enjoyed each other's company. When Eddie suddenly told friends that he and Vera were getting married soon, a "very pissed-off" Vera took the initiative to dig into his past. What she found was that he'd already been married and divorced three times, and, after nosing around, she came to believe Eddie was a closeted homosexual. Vera convinced him that he needed to be honest with himself and her, and they decided to marry. Life with Eddie would enable Vera to get her son, Tony, who adored Eddie, back into the suburbs, and give him a better life.

Vera "behaved" herself while she was married to Eddie. "I lived the image that was expected of me, for Tony's benefit. Now he [Eddie] was having a great old time!" They were together for ten years before Eddie died. "It was a great arrangement. It solved his problem, and it provided me with an escort when I needed one. And he was a great male influence for Tony."

When Eddie died, Vera realized it was time for her to live who she was, and within weeks, she came out to her son and told him about changes she wanted to make in her life. Asking if he was going to be okay with it, Tony told her, "If that's what you want to do, and that's going to make you happy, then I think you should do it." Having come out as a lesbian, Vera added gay and lesbian causes to the long, long list of outlets for her activism, but she remained an outspoken voice that demanded to be heard for other causes as well.

Living who she really was, Vera found herself at a New Year's party with a woman she'd been dating for three months. Vera felt practically alone since

Vera and Juan

her date was busy flirting with everybody in the room. But something good did come out of it; people she'd met at that party later introduced her to Juan. After a faltering start, Vera and Juan were soon spending all their spare time either together or on the phone. In 1975, Vera and Juan had a commitment ceremony at the MCC church, and moved in together.

Moving day brought Vera her first exposure to Juan's temper. She remembers thinking, "If I could have put everything I needed into a red or green hankie, and put it on the end of a bamboo pole, I would've left!" They got past that first problem, but Juan would periodically explode in jealousy over things that meant nothing. It might be an innocent phone conversation with a gardener, or things over which Vera had no control, like someone flirting with her. This went on for years. In 1985, Vera was approaching retirement, and was still living with Juan.

> *I knew that if I retired I was not going to be able to live in that house. [Juan] was an RN and she worked nights. That meant I had to creep around like a mouse, too quiet all day, so she could sleep, and wait on her hand and foot. ... She's going to want to control my every waking moment. She'd done things like go to work at night and have this overwhelming sense of insecurity, leave her job, abandon her nurse station, and drive home. And I'm asleep, and when I look up she's standing over me. Scared the hell out of me! ...I was not going to be able to involve myself in any of the activities that I was accustomed to. I had always been an activist. And I knew that [creeping around like a mouse] was gonna kill me in no time.*

Vera knew she had to leave. She didn't have a plan as to how it would happen, but she didn't have to wait long for an opportunity to present itself. During dinner one night, Juan "lost her temper and threw the plate and got food all over the kitchen walls. And I was hell-bent not to clean it up."

Vera calmly left to lie down in another room, and Juan followed, nearly busting down the door with her fist. "She wanted to know who the hell I thought I was closing the door! After all, that was her house!" Deciding to leave, Vera threw a few changes of clothing in a suitcase so she could go to work and, after a show-down at the door, left. But it wasn't a clean break. It took years for the relationship to truly come to an end.

Juan was still in and out of Vera's life years later; Vera had tried hard to find some way to make it work between them. In 1997, Vera had moved to Arizona. She loved Arizona, but she didn't look forward to living alone, so Vera agreed to let Juan move in with her, and they tried to make it work once again. Before long, Vera realized that there wasn't any hope and, with the help of friends, she managed to send Juan and all her belongings back to California.

In 1993

I had never, in any relationship in my lifetime, worked so hard to make one work, as I did with her. ... The 4th of February, 1997, was my date of independence and freedom. And by the next day, my face was totally different. Everybody noticed it.

Vera was very involved with the Black Gay and Lesbian Leadership Forum, serving as a member of its Board of Directors. She was instrumental in the formation of Old Lesbians Organizing for Change (OLOC). During this busy time in her life, Vera was also involved with the National Gay and Lesbian Task Force.

Working with the American Society on Aging (ASA) posed an interesting set of circumstances. Even though their focus was improving the lives of older adults, it became evident that the ASA itself was ageist. When the organization turned a blind eye to the problem, Vera and her friends (Jean Adelman, Phyllis Lyon, Del Martin, Shevy Healy, Dottie Fowler, and Ruth Silver) caused such a controversy about their policies that the ASA formed an auxiliary organization to address the issues of aging GLBT people.

At 77, almost fifteen years after retirement, with a host of great and great-great-grandchildren, Vera continues to "stir the pot," speaking and organizing around many issues including, but certainly not limited to, racism and ageism.

As Vera succinctly states, "We are a project in progress."

Vera continues to live in Arizona.
Interviewer: Arden Eversmeyer

Jean
Mountaingrove

Born October 1925 in Iowa
Interviewed in 2003 at age 78

At one particular moment, I did that.

A social worker with two marriages behind her, and two teenaged children, Jean experienced a pivotal event in her mid-40s. She was invited to a women's conference in Philadelphia, and found herself in an informal meeting of a dozen women. After telling a personal story, the discussion leader said, "Now we'll go around the room and each women will talk about some woman she has loved in her life. Maybe it's your teacher, your mother, your grandmother ..." Hearing this, Jean was overwhelmed with memories and a startling realization.

> *Click, click, click, click, click. I fell in love in the third grade with my music teacher. ... I used to take violets to her at school and leave them at her door, and four leaf clovers that I would find on the way to school. When she got married, it broke my heart. I fell in love with my nursery school supervisor, the minister's*

wife. ... I sent Valentines with no names on them.

I went to graduate school in social work. I fell in love with my supervisor there. And I think I tried to take flowers to her door, you know, anonymously. But I never knew the word "lesbian." So when I spoke with my graduate advisor about having a unique relationship, she paused, and then changed the subject. We were on the campus there, talking.

Jean at 4 years old

And she said she could be in touch with me after I graduated that summer, but she never got in touch with me. I did, several times, go and park across the street from her house, in case I could see her coming and going.

I decided, after all those clicks, that I had potential to be a lesbian — maybe a history of being a lesbian!

That was an unsettling time for Jean. By 1970, she had been married twice, and both times she'd been in love. She'd left her second husband, and unsure what was next for her and her kids, spent nine months living at a Quaker center. While there, Jean began investigating life in a commune.

I heard of this one in Oregon called Mountain Grove, that was supposed to be spiritual, drug-and-alcohol-free, and educational. I came up with the kids to visit, and I fell in love with the land.

I wandered the land, walked up the valley, and on one of those times I came upon a small grove of trees in a larger meadow. I discovered that I felt different in that grove of trees. I knew nothing about tree hugging. I did not know that there was anybody else in the world — you know, how can we think that we are the only one who knows something out of all the millions of people? But, being lonely, I put my arms around one of the larger trees and just put my cheek against the tree. I felt such a profound peacefulness. I described it as a sense of "anything I did was all right — nothing was there that I had to do." In other words, it was unconditional love.

Jean was at peace with her decision to make this major change in her life, and decided to join the commune despite being a decade or two older than almost every other member. Another hurdle was that Jean's kids were teenagers. Her son, who suffered with dyslexia, stayed with Jean, and some of the men helped her teach him what he needed to know. Her daughter went back to school with the Quakers.

Not long after she'd settled into her new life, her ex-husband came to visit. When Jean wouldn't let him share her quarters, he headed across the road, where he quickly became involved with another commune woman. When he decided to stay and marry the other woman, Jean called to commiserate with Ruth, a friend in Philadelphia. Ruth wanted Jean to come back East, but Jean couldn't stand the thought of returning to the smog. "Why don't you come here?" Jean asked.

"When Ruth came, I showed her where [the grove of trees] was. And she didn't think I was crazy at all." Walking back from a meeting one evening, Jean's life took a turn.

Ruth and I went for a walk up the road. Well, one thing led to you know what! She said that she loved me, and wanted to live with me. And I thought that was wonderful, 'cause I was lonely. And then we went back to the cabin. And we decided that if our sleeping bags zipped together, we'd spend the night together. Well, they did... and we did.

We did not come out directly to the community, but it certainly became very obvious. As a friend of mine said, "We're not out, we're obvious."

Jean and Ruth soon said to each other, "We've got to find the lesbians." They began attending Quaker meetings in Eugene and Portland. The Quakers had taken a stand in support of lesbian and gay people.

Ruth was a writer, and they began submitting articles to a local newspaper called *Eugene Women's Press*.

> *I sent mine in as Jean Ex Mountaingrove, meaning 'out of Mountain Grove'. … When I first saw my name in print in* Women's Press, *I cried. It was a changing point in my life. I now felt that I could speak to the public. It was not just my journal and my friends. I was out there.*

Elated as she was, there was a downside to having her articles published. Jean and Ruth were now, unequivocally, "out" in the commune. They were given two weeks to leave. "We were thrown out of Mountain Grove for being lesbian." Gay men in a community nearby said we could live there. They had a 10-by-10 cabin up on a hill. It was a meditation center. It had no door or insulation, but it had one window, and it had a place for a little tin stove."

Jean and Ruth weren't sure it was the right place for them, so they began an odyssey up and down the West Coast, to look for other options that might suit their needs.

In 1974, they settled briefly in Mendocino, California, where they worked with other women on a magazine called *Country Women*. "It was a women's commune, really. And they did this magazine—they'd done it for maybe five or six months or more." They did an *I Ching* reading and received the message "Pushing Upwards: Supreme Success." As Jean and Ruth helped with the magazine, and continued to think about what came next, they felt guided to do a magazine on the subject of women's spirituality.

> *We learned that three women had just bought land outside of Grant's Pass [a mountainous area of southwest Oregon]. They were feminists. We thought they were lesbians. And they were very interested in doing a feminist project. They had just moved in, had been in city feminism, and were ready, gung ho, to do something.*

Out of this shared interest came a new women's collective named Womanshare. Deciding to start their own magazine was the easy step. Next came the hard part:

> We sent out the word in every way we could that we wanted material, and all the local women were invited to write for it. We set ourselves a goal that we'd come out quarterly for the equinoxes and solstices.
>
> We wanted it to be a reliable institution because there was a women's magazine from back East that just suddenly stopped. ... We said we were not going to do that. We're going to prove that women can be responsible and on time.
>
> It was August, and it was time to get it out. And we didn't have any electricity or an electric typewriter. So we could go over to Womanshare, where they had electricity, and we rented the electric typewriter and started in.

Everyone pitched in, including a woman traveler who happened to have her own typewriter. The next hurdle was the expense of having it printed and mailed.

> We didn't have any money. Ruth had sent out several requests for funding. Ruth is working class, and she has a different attitude about money, and she could ask for it. ... She sent out these letters, and we were a little concerned that it was getting kind of close, and we didn't know what was going to happen. She hadn't gotten any answers. So we did an I-Ching reading. It said, "Abundance." So she got in her car and went to the Wolf Creek Post Office

Example of artwork in **WomanSpirit**

[to check their post office box]. She came back with a check for
$2,000.

We went up [to the printers] and slept on the floor in our
sleeping bags and, with the help of local women, worked on
collating, stapling, and trimming 2000 copies of the magazine.
We took it to the women's bookstore, Mother Kali's in Eugene,
and to the first Fall Gathering that was here, out by Ashland
that year. And then, we were off!

WomanSpirit, focusing on women's artwork, photographs,
songs, stories, articles, discussions, poems, letters, and book
reviews, was underway. The magazine was a reflection of Jean's
belief in the value of people speaking and sharing their own truth.
It also reflected her strong belief in feminism.

For five years, Jean and Ruth lived in that 10-by-10 cabin that
had been offered to them by the gay men.

It had room for a double bed and about 18 inches of space at
the foot of the bed … in which we put up a shelf. That was our
business desk! And that coincided with the front edge of the bed.
Then the rest of the maybe four, or three feet of space, was the
kitchen. We had two cups, two bowls, two spoons, a little area
for the tin stove, and then the doorway.

By the time Jean and Ruth moved away, they had managed
to actually have a door in the opening, and the gay men had made
them a stained glass window. They had also managed to string
a tarp to form a shelter outdoors for an outdoor kitchen, and
convert a chicken house space for wood storage, file cabinets and
photography equipment.

The arrangement didn't last long, though, and years later they
were declared "man-haters" and asked to leave. They had heard
that a nearby piece of land, known as Rootworks, was to be sold
and, although it was described as a "rag-tag scrap of land", they
purchased it, and moved into one of the two existing structures,
taking with them their door and stained glass window.

Jean and Ruth worried that they'd run into more people who
objected to their lifestyle in their new location. To head off any

Jean on right, building a cabin in 1979

problems, they made a concerted effort to get out and visit their neighbors. After turning down offers of coffee, cigarettes, and beer, they were quickly deemed to be "schoolteacher types and terribly boring, and of no consequence whatsoever."

Living at Rootworks gave Jean and Ruth plenty of learning opportunities. Although they didn't know much about construction, with some help, they put a porch on their home, and built another small cabin and a barn. The barn was an overly ambitious project, but they did end up with space to house everything necessary for producing their magazine, as well as space for a photography lab for Ruth.

Lack of electricity was a problem that Ruth managed to solve. She discovered that, with a car battery (which they could recharge at the local gas station) and an inverter, they could run an electric typewriter.

Photography was another important facet of their lives, and they were soon hosting events with that subject, and producing another publication, *The Blatant Image*.

Ruth's interests became more and more focused on their second publication, and Jean found herself struggling to keep *WomanSpirit* going on her own. They had started *WomanSpirit* with eight subscriptions and, after ten years, had gained 800; they had also placed it in more than a hundred bookstores. The work was inspiring, but it was also crushing. Once it was put together, it went to the printer. When it was ready, the women hand-wrote the labels, packaged the magazines, and sent them out. Exactly 10 years after it began, Jean and Ruth had reached their limit, and quit publishing *WomanSpirit*.

Soon after the magazine was discontinued, one more building that they had constructed got a new use when Jean and Ruth decided to separate.

I moved into what was the shop. And it still had all the saws hanging on the wall, and all the tools along another wall. We added a greenhouse on the front of that building, facing south, and an outdoor kitchen, which was originally a woodshed, on the north side.

Jean continued to live at Rootworks. Ruth moved on, coming back to visit occasionally. They had vowed that they would not sell the land for their own advantage, since so many women had contributed to its existence. Together they had the property set up as a land trust for women.

Various women came and went on the land during the next few years. Personalities clashed, and Jean opted for an extended stay in a nearby town. But she couldn't let it go. Rootworks was a part of her. Jean was very comfortable living where she was, but Rootworks was home to her spirit.

There were many questions about the future of Rootworks and other pieces of women's land in the area, so Jean helped organize a gathering of women who had financial and legal responsibility for the land. Out of the meeting came a new commitment to ensure the option of living on women's land stays viable, and Jean feels more hopeful about the future.

One of the concerns the group addressed was aging—both meeting the different needs of aging women, and making sure that as women age everyone continues to listen to them.

Jean has never been one to sit back and complain about what is happening. Instead, she encourages people to act. Attending the first conference for old lesbians in California, Jean found herself listening to a group of women lamenting the fact that the event wasn't political enough for them. Speaking up, she said, "We can do whatever we want. We can just call a meeting about that." Spurred on, the group did call a meeting at which Barbara Macdonald (renowned for challenging ageism within the feminist movement) spoke. Out of this initial meeting grew OLOC, which is now celebrating its 20th year.

"I was only a spark in that. But you know, at one particular moment, I did that, and other women did the work to bring it forward today."

Jean continues to live at Rootworks in Oregon.
Interviewer: Gloria Stancich

Arminta 'Skip' Neal

Born August 1921 in Texas
Interviewed in 2001 at age 80

Come, come ... kiss the crone.

Skip really enjoyed the lakes, mountains, and campfires, but what she really loved about camping as a child was that it was one of the few occasions when she didn't have to dress up. "Growing up, I was supposed to be a southern lady." Skip relished the opportunity to run around in jeans, and play in the dirt and water, frustrating her mother.

Many of Skip's childhood memories show just how different she was from the average "southern lady." She clearly recalls Christmas morning when she was five. All she wanted was a truck and a pocketknife.

I came down the stairs into the living room, and here was a little red roadster. And I cried and cried because I couldn't understand how Santa could have gotten it so wrong. I wanted a dump truck, you know. And my mother ... couldn't quite

see her little girl going up and down the street in front of
the house in a dump truck. Little girls were not supposed to
have pocketknives. But dolls? Oh, I got dolls, and I took them
apart. ... [Mother] would make lovely little clothes for the dolls,
and I'd take them off and try to find out what made them work.

By the time Skip reached high school age, she knew she was
truly different from her friends.

I've known all my life that I was a lesbian. I didn't know what
to call it in those days. I knew I was different. I knew. I can't
remember a time that I didn't know. I was not going to marry
and have kids.

Skip also knew she was going to have to support herself.
Growing up in the Los Angeles area, she spent her first few college
years at the University of California at Los Angeles majoring in
Fine Arts. During her junior year, Pearl Harbor was bombed. "I
wanted desperately to enlist, but my folks convinced me to finish
college."

Skip struggled with what she was going to do as an art major,
but she stayed in school. She knew she didn't want to teach high
school, and didn't think she was good enough to make a living
as a commercial artist. Her thoughts kept on going back to all
the Saturdays she spent at the Natural History museum as a kid,
and she decided she wanted to become a scientific illustrator.
"Somebody has to draw the pots and the bones and the arrow-
heads that they collect ... and I can do that."

World War II was raging, and in order to speed up the process
of building planes, artists were recruited to make mathematically
correct perspective drawings.

The government came on campus recruiting art majors. It was
going to be a six-week-long class, and it was to be held in the
Art Center in Los Angeles. This was a school that I had yearned
to go to, but my folks couldn't afford it.

So I thought, "Well, that would be good training for
scientific illustration, and I get to go to the Art Center while I

take it." The only proviso was that if you were offered a job in the defense industry by the time the class had ended, you had to take it to repay the government.

Skip looked at the job as an opportunity, and took the training. She went to work for Douglas Aircraft doing technical drawings in the hydraulics section, "which is like trying to draw spaghetti in perspective!" She loved it, but was still anxious to enlist.

As soon as she was laid off from Douglas, Skip joined the Women's Ambulance and Defense Corps, a civilian support organization. While it wasn't the WACs, it did fulfil her desire to wear a uniform, and allowed her to continue with her schooling.

In 1944, she finally got her chance and became a WAC. She was stationed near Washington, D.C. Skip was eligible to go to Officer's Candidate School, but she thought "I'd better not try to be an officer until I know what it's like to be an enlisted person." Becoming part of the Signal Battalion ensured she'd stay stationed near D.C., where she could spend her free time exploring the area and visiting the museums.

As a WAC, age 24

Skip loved being a WAC, and loved being stationed near D.C. She didn't have a personal life, but then she met someone. "That was my first physical experience — sexual experience. I thought, 'Well, this is what I was supposed to have been feeling for the fellows all this time.'" For the most part, getting caught with her girlfriend wasn't a big fear since they only had six months left to go. They were on different bases and whenever they got together off-base, they wore civvies (civilian clothes).

I don't know what would have happened if we had been in longer, or if we'd both been on the same base. I think I would

*have been in trouble. I think I would have been in deep
trouble! Because I was, you know, this was my first "head over
heels" experience.*

At the end of her two-year hitch, she and her lover, Mac, left
the WACs and drove back to the West Coast.

Skip was eligible for GI benefits and went back to school,
while Mac got a job. "We started going to parties with the art
students, and it turns out she [Mac] was bisexual." When Mac
married, it just about killed Skip.

She returned to her professional schooling at the long-desired
Art Center in Los Angeles, but Skip was disappointed to discover
that if she wanted to continue in the program, she would be
required to take fashion design. Her heart was still set on scientific
illustration, so she quit art school and began canvassing museums
all over the country, looking for a job.

Working as a scientific illustrator

Her determination paid off when Skip landed a position at a museum in Denver, on the requirement that she would attend the local university, as part of her job, and study anthropology. At the museum, Skip was fortunate to work for Eric Douglas, a world-class authority on historic Native American material. Color photographs weren't reliable at this time, and Skip was one of four artists who spent much of their time painting small watercolors of artifacts on their index cards. Her boss also involved Skip in every aspect of creating displays for museums.

The Natural History Museum in Denver was Skip's home for the next 32 years. For 25 of those years, she designed exhibits. For the last seven years, Skip served as the Assistant Director. During her tenure, she was integrally involved in the formation of a Native American Advisory Council that was given oversight authority on how the Museum treated and displayed Native American cultural artifacts. It wasn't until years later that federal laws were passed mandating similar guidelines. Skip had shown the foresight to involve the Native American community from the outset, and the Denver museum avoided untold expenses that would have been required to redesign their displays.

Visitors from other museums quickly recognized that Skip had developed several innovative ways to deal with logistical problems, such as integrating false walls that allowed access to displays for cleaning and maintenance. In response to constant requests for information on her innovations, Skip created illustrations and instructions that were later published as two books: *Exhibits for the Small Museum: A Handbook* and *Help! For the Small Museum: A Handbook of Exhibit Ideas and Methods*.

Representing the museum, Skip sat listening to an elaborate presentation at an annual meeting of the American Association of Museums, and grew more frustrated as each minute passed.

These guys got up to talk about how to build exhibits for museums. … Their whole premise was that you can't do it; you don't have the training, so don't try. What you should do is "hire us, and we will come and do a consultation with you." Well, their consultation fee was, a lot of times, as much as a

small museum's annual budget. I sat there just getting steamed.
Finally, when they got through, and were asking for comments
from the audience, I screwed up my courage and stood up.

My whole body was shaking because I was so scared. But I
was pissed. I thought these guys needed to be taken down a peg
or two. I said their presentation had been very interesting, but
if they would check the bulletin boards in the entrance to the
lecture hall, to see what was available in terms of positions and
salaries being paid, they would note that their fees were consid-
erably more than most small museums' budgets. And I found
it upsetting to infer that people didn't have the intelligence to
create their own exhibits!

The speakers meekly thanked her for her comments, and Skip
sat down to a great round of applause.

By the time Skip neared retirement age, she was considered a
world-class authority on building displays in small museums. She
was often sought out to share her expertise. In 1981, at the request
of the Nigerian government, she took an extended leave-of-
absence from the Denver Museum, and taught a course in Nigeria
on creating and maintaining museum exhibits. Although she had
been offered the option of staying in a local hotel and being driven
to and fro daily, Skip opted to get a broader experience by staying
in the spartan student quarters: leaky roof, mosquitoes, lack of
hot water, colorful lizards, and all. As fascinating as it was, Skip
was relieved to have an excuse not to return, when they asked her
again, a few years later.

While living and working in Denver, Skip joined the Women's
Marine Corps Reserve and met a woman.

In those days you thought you had to have a partner. That
was what you did. There were two women [in the Reserve] in
a relationship, but it was really rocky. I became friends with
them. It just kind of happened that one of them decided she'd
like to move in with me. And I thought, 'Well, that's pretty nice.'
They had some really abusive things in their relationship. So
she moved in with me, and we were together 21 years. Then she
found someone else and moved out.

Skip was only 55, and had gotten used to having someone around, so she felt she needed to seek out another relationship. Looking to connect with other women, Skip joined several organizations, but didn't find anyone else that interested her.

It took me a long time to get used to living by myself. ... It would be wonderful to be in a committed relationship, but it would have to be someone who had their own home. ... I'm set in my ways. I'm a pack rat.

Skip didn't come out at work until the day she retired. "Had I been out during my working time, I would have been fired. And while I was partnered (my partner was an elementary school teacher), she would have been fired." After coming out to a couple of people at her retirement party, Skip decided to tell her physician, whose response was "Well, I knew that the day you came in." Even after joining an almost exclusively lesbian women's chorus, she continued to be very cautious about coming out.

Art was an important part of Skip's life. She was always sketching and drawing cartoons while in the WACs, and later on during archeological digs. At 65, she put that talent to work again. She had been working with a therapist, and found herself wondering about the aging process.

The analyst I happened to work with was Clarissa Pinkola Estés. ... I started working with her, and one day these two women fell out of the end of my pen. I knew immediately these two women were my tribal elders.

The drawings that Skip later described as "two naked old women just having a 'whoee' of a time" went on to be featured under the title *Tribal Elders* in several feminist publications.

After decades of worrying about who might know, or even suspect, she was a lesbian, Skip retired and boldly wrote to her congressional representatives, outing herself as an ex-military old lesbian and urging them to support gay rights. She even found herself marching in the Pride parade in New York. "They had a car for some of us older folks. But I rode in the car for about the first mile, and I couldn't stand it. I had to get out and walk!"

A year or so after retirement, Skip met with a young man who knew of her work. He asked if she was interested in going to Peru to teach on a Fulbright scholarship. She lacked the customary Ph.D., or any ability to speak the native language, yet Skip was awarded the scholarship. She spent three months teaching and consulting near Lima.

Skip felt strongly that she wanted to put any money she had to good use, especially since she was a single woman without any family that could inherit.

Since I'm not partnered, and since I have no family, a few years ago I got to thinking, "What happens when I die?" You don't want the state to take this and build new jails with it.

So while she was involved with the women's chorus, Skip financed a couple of competitions for women composers, and this led to one of the most meaningful events in her life.

Skip had met the composer, Kay Gardner, on an earlier trip to the sacred sights of England and Ireland. She greatly admired Kay's work, which used music for healing. Skip had been exposed to different cultural rituals during her years studying anthropology, and found herself thinking:

In our culture, we've lost the rituals that go with women's rites of passage. We're christened, and we have weddings, and we have funerals. But nobody celebrates the first time we menstruate. Nobody celebrates menopause.

I didn't have enough [money] to do a full commission, but I asked Kay Gardner if she would be interested in writing a piece of music that would recreate the rites of passage of a woman's life. And she did a magnificent thing. It turned out to be Ouroboros… an oratorio that involves a forty-piece orchestra, a hundred-voice chorus, and six vocalists ranging from a little girl to a crone. And she asked me to sing the part of the crone. It premiered in 1994 at the National Women's Music Festival in Indiana. Of course, I'm prejudiced, but I think it's an absolutely beautiful piece of music. And the words are powerful.

Ouroboros premiered to a full house at the 20th anniversary of the NWMF. Other than performing the part of the crone for the performance, Skip hadn't shared with many that she had had a role in creating the oratario. Shortly before the piece was to be performed, Clarissa Pinkola Estés told her "If they want to identify you, you let them identify you, sister. For two thousand years, the culture has tried to hide any source of [women's] creativity, or sponsorship, or whatever." At the end of the performance, Kay Gardner said, "I want to introduce the woman whose idea this was. She gave me the seed money to get it started," and she called Skip to the stage.

> *The orchestra and the chorus gasped. They hadn't known. ... I was walking up the aisle to the lobby afterwards, and some woman stopped me and said, "Oh, I think it's just so wonderful when women of means support women's projects."*

After clarifying that she was not "a woman of means," Skip told her, "I saved money for at least five years, because I knew there would be some woman's project come along that I would want to support. This was it. Anybody can do it."

Skip had been profoundly moved by *Ouroboros* and the role she played in making it happen, and that led her to think further about what was going to happen when she died. Her answer was to establish "Skip's Sappho Fund," to support lesbian creativity. Once that idea hit her, she realized she didn't have to wait until she died to start the project; that money she wanted to go for this purpose could go into a fund and grow until her death. After saving for three years to accumulate $10,000, Skip contacted Astraea [Lesbian Foundation for Justice], and worked with them to set up the fund with the guideline that grants be given directly to individuals. She set a few stipulations:

> *I told them I wanted it set up for areas west of the Mississippi, because people in the east have access to so many resources. And right now I'm excluding Texas and California, mainly because I'm pissed at [President George W.] Bush, and California is so open, I feel people in California have access to*

a lot of money and a lot of things without having to be worried about being identified as being a lesbian.

The grants might not be any more than $500, ... but I think the validation of getting something will let them know that they're on the right track, that their creativity is at least being acknowledged.

To celebrate her 70th birthday, Skip and friends had spent time sketching and painting near Taos. As she neared 75, friends all pitched in to turn her backyard into a groomed garden for a party. And when her 80th rolled around, friends told her not to worry, they wanted to arrange a gathering on her behalf at the local music school. When her friends came to pick her up to take her to the celebration, Skip was astounded that they arrived in a limousine with champagne in hand.

Of course, as with almost every other aspect of Skip's life, music was a big part of the celebration. She was flabbergasted when the festivities had to be interrupted for her to take a phone call. It was from Kay Gardner.

Later, while *Ouroboros* was playing in the background, some-
one hushed the crowd so they could all hear the lyrics, "Come, come... kiss the crone," which, of course, they did.

Skip Neal died in 2003. Interviewer: Arden Eversmeyer

Self sketch done by Skip in 2001

Ocie Perry

Born July 1926 in Arkansas
Interviewed in 2003 at age 77

There's nothing wrong with what I feel.

Growing up in the town of Hot Springs, Arkansas, during the school year, and in the nearby countryside during the summers, Ocie Perry got to experience both worlds. Life in the country included tagging along with her siblings, skinny-dipping in the local creek, learning how to track rabbits, harvesting home-grown fruits and nuts, and lots of fresh air. Life in the city, however, was a drastically different experience.

> *I found myself much happier on the farm than I was in the city, because when you went to the city kids teased you about being "country"… teased you about talking different.… And yet, my father always told us that we were just as smart as they were, or smarter, and to not let that bother us. But it used to really bother me to have kids tease me about being "country." Sometimes we didn't dress just like they did, things like that.*

Ocie worked as a bath attendant at the famous Arkansas Springs during her teens.

> *I used to bathe people and make good money, because they tipped you really well. I even had an opportunity to bathe Ava Gardner, who was a [movie] star. It was so funny. She wanted to take me home with her as a maid, and I was highly insulted that she would ask me. ... I said, "I'm going to be a nurse!" as if that wasn't a maid. But nursing to me was a profession. And I was insulted that she could only see having me as a maid, and I let her know!*

Ava Gardner later apologized, and wished her well.

Ocie was attending high school in Little Rock when she met and married a young man. Her mother and father said she was getting too close to this boy, and even though they knew the young man's family, they worried about her. "You just didn't get pregnant if you were my age in that day and time, so they said, 'Go ahead and get married.' They had to sign a paper for us to get married because I was underage. I was sixteen, and he was twenty-three."

Married life took Ocie away from Arkansas for the first time ever. The young couple moved to Omaha, where Ocie was still too young to get a job that she wanted, so she worked as a butcher, falling back on skills she'd picked up during her country life.

World War II had broken out when Ocie turned eighteen, and she was able to get a better job. She was now "Ocie the Riveter."

> *I worked there until my husband, Ralph, came back in 1945. My marriage was not a marriage because I didn't even know what I was doing in the first place. I didn't know what love was about either, but I thought I was in love. I really tried to live as a wife, even with him overseas, but when he came back we were strangers to each other, because he had changed. I was nineteen when he got back. He still cared for me; I didn't care for him anymore. He looked strange to me. He didn't look like the same guy. And I knew what had happened was that I was in love with the uniform. ... And I was in love with Ralph as a football star.*

Ocie struggled to live up to what she felt was her obligation to be a good wife. Ralph was restless. He didn't like Omaha, so he and Ocie moved to Chicago.

"When we got there, I started seeing a real difference in Ralph. He was drinking more than he was doing anything else." Ocie came to realize that he was being haunted by his experiences in the war, and suffered from depression. She tried several times to get Ralph to go to the VA hospital for help, but he just wouldn't go.

Ocie at 18

In one of his many drinking episodes, Ralph killed himself. He'd struggled with suicidal thoughts for awhile, but always felt better the next day. Ocie clearly remembers telling him, "Why don't you just go to sleep, you're just drinking. Tomorrow morning you'll be okay." She found him dead in the morning. "I live with a lot of guilt about that, because I felt I let him do it." Ocie knew she had tried to get him to seek help, but some of Ralph's family blamed her. It was only with help from her father that Ocie came to accept that she had done what she could, and she wasn't responsible.

Ocie was galvanized into turning her life around. She went to Detroit and finished high school. "They thought I was a faculty member when I was in the school, because I was wearing stockings and shoes. The rest of them were wearing socks, and I was twenty-three years old!" Diploma in hand, Ocie went on to enroll as the first African-American student at St. Mary's School of Nursing in Kankakee, Illinois. Being accepted wasn't a given. It was only after she pointed out her determination (evidenced by going back to high school), and her scholastic records, that the board decided to accept her. But even with her determination, nursing school was not a smooth ride. One of the classes nursing students were required to take was a six-week course in dietetics.

> *I had to work in the kitchen, and she [the nun in charge] told Sister Mary that she didn't want me in there; that she had never had a Black in the kitchen. One day, I wanted to show her that I had prepared a tray for diabetics, and I wanted to get her thoughts about it. She looked down at the tray and just took her hand and flung it clear across the room. I hadn't put one thing on the tray, the substitute sugar.*

Demanding Ocie do the tray over, the nun didn't even tell her what she'd done wrong. "That's the first time I ever felt like I wanted to kill somebody." Sister Mary managed to calm Ocie, who had decided to quit and go home. "You didn't come here to leave because of something like this." That was just one of many unique situations Ocie had to deal with while in nursing school.

At graduation, Ocie's mom surprised her by saying, "One thing I want you to do before you leave here, I want you to go and thank her for making you a great nurse, because you'll always know how to set up a diabetic tray!" In her cap and gown, Ocie approached her nemesis and said, "I came to thank you." "Thank me?" the nun said. "Yes. For making it really tough for me." The nun didn't apologize but was obviously moved by what Ocie had said. Appreciating what her mother had urged her to do, Ocie says, "the experience taught me that this is the best way to handle evil, with kindness rather than with meanness."

After a brief stint working as an ER nurse in Hot Springs, Ocie searched out an opportunity to move from the South. "It was still bigotry, you know, a separation, a hospital for the blacks and one for the whites." Ocie moved to Cleveland to escape the oppressive South. There she both worked and pursued a bachelor's degree in nursing.

Ocie dated men from time to time, but she also began to realize she had to deal with her different feelings about women. "I would right away go, 'This is silly. That's crazy. Why am I thinking like this?' ... I knew something was different about me when I was nine years old, because I had a crush on my brother's girlfriend."

She sought out counseling about her unsettling feelings, and when Ocie told the psychologist she knew what she felt was wrong, citing the Bible as her authority, he challenged her. "What God are you talking about?... God is love! Why would He not want you to love?" Still, she struggled. Seeking out the help of another professional, Ocie was again told, "Just be you, instead of trying to be someone else." Dating yet another man, a young doctor, she found herself sitting at dinner with him and realizing all her thoughts were about Marion, a woman she was attracted to.

"I made a decision right then at that dinner... to go and let her know how I felt. 'This is it. I've got to stop pretending.'" Her date dropped her off at the dorm, where both she and Marion lived, and Ocie went straight to Marion's room. Marion was sitting in the dark, and invited her in, leaving the lights off. "'I want you to just come and sit down, and you tell me why you're here.'" Ocie answered, "I don't know. I just keep thinking about you. And tonight I was on this date, and I didn't want to be with him anymore." When Marion said she felt the same way, and Ocie asked what they were going to do about it, Ocie spent the night.

Working together presented some problems to Ocie and Marion. They could hardly keep their eyes off each other or the smiles off their faces.

One night, after going out to a movie so they could be alone, Ocie and Marion decided to drive to a nearby park to spend some time together.

> Just park, and just sit out there and talk and look at the moon, and just talk. But we ended up kissin' again, huggin' again, kissin', and we got really carried away again. And the next thing you knew, a big flashlight was shining into the car. And we looked, and it was a cop, and he said, "I don't know what you ladies call yourselves doing, and it's none of my business, but you're going to have to get out of here. You can't stay here to do it." We were so scared. We didn't even say "yes sir, okay," or nothing, we just looked startled, because he put the light right on us. But he was nice enough to get in his car and drive off after making those remarks. And we got out of there!

Ocie and Marion were truly frightened by the close call. They were afraid that they might be risking their jobs. Out of fear, they pledged to be much more circumspect.

A move to Detroit came next. Her mother was ill, so Ocie decided she and Marion would both transfer jobs and buy a home where her mother could live with them. But Marion still had a boyfriend that she just couldn't seem to let go of, who was trailing along behind her. Ocie finally had to make the decision for them. "I felt like she wasn't as ready as me, because she was still trying to please him, and she didn't want him to know, and she didn't want her mother and her family to know. ... She was confused about it." Ocie told Marion she had to do what she felt was right for herself, and they split up. Marion went on to marry, but, by now, Ocie knew without question that she was a lesbian.

Grieving the loss of her relationship, and hating the cold in Michigan, Ocie moved herself and her mother to San Francisco. She had been working for the VA in Michigan and was offered a job transfer. Ocie continued working for the VA for another thirteen years.

Not one to let what she perceived as a wrong go unchallenged, Ocie was often in the middle of public demonstrations, bringing attention to poor working conditions within the VA for patients, and organizing the nursing staff.

Ocie's interest in the VA system was not just as an employee. She had also joined the Army Nurse Corps Reserve Unit. She served as a Captain for six years. And she did change things. Ocie's willingness to stand up for what she knew what was right contributed to revamping the existing hospital, building a new one, and changing employment policies for the nursing staff so that they would receive overtime, vacation time, sick days, and

Army Nurse Corps, age 36

other benefits. "I felt I'd done what I needed to do and it was time for me to leave and go somewhere else."

A single woman taking care of an ailing mother, Ocie wasn't interested in any more complications. But then a baby came into her life. A friend told her of a baby waiting to be adopted, and insisted Ocie go visit the child. She was smitten, and immediately started working to adopt the baby girl. Ocie's lawyer told her, "You're a working woman, you're buying your own home. There's no excuse."

TV debut at 62 years of age

Even with the lawyer's assurances, Ocie felt fortunate her sexual orientation never came up. "It probably would have been a big deal, but then nobody assumed anything." At 41, Ocie became a mother.

She had developed an interest in working in radio, and had taken some training. This led to a weekend job as a DJ at Peg's Place, a lesbian bar. "I didn't plan on it. It just happened." Before Ocie, they'd never had a woman DJ, even though it was a lesbian bar! Her radio training also led to her own call-in TV music show called *Jazz in the City*. Hosting her show fed a part of her that had always wanted to be a musician. She loved both of her part-time jobs, but when her health started to suffer, she gave up the DJ job.

Ocie then began another career, joining the Postal Service as head nurse, and her reputation came with her. She hadn't been there long before other nurses were asking for her help in organizing. But she had her mother, and a child to care for, and her television show; she didn't want to get involved. "They knew, if they kept on coming and telling me enough ... when they told me that janitors got more [pay than they did]."

She gave in and got involved. Even though she had insisted that she would only help the nurses organize, and not run the effort, Ocie was voted their president. Feeling pressure from her other obligations in life, Ocie came up with a solution. The nurses would affiliate as a branch of the Mail Handlers Union, instead of forming their own. After successfully shepherding them through this process, and working with union executives in Washington, D.C., Ocie again wanted to go back to her other responsibilities. No matter how she tried, though, she kept on being dragged back into it. Work with the Postal Service and the union consumed her attention for years to come.

Ocie had a yearning to get away from the city. She retired after 33 years of civil service, and after having lost her mother, she bought a little house near the Mojave Desert.

> I always enjoyed creating things, so I went and renovated this whole house, had new carpets put in and fenced it in. And there was where I really needed to be. I gained a certain relationship with myself, because at that time I had had relationships as a lesbian, but none of them had materialized the way I thought they should. So I was enjoying some time for myself: some time for reflection and just looking at me.
>
> I'm really enjoying myself, but at the same time, I'm running across situations where they need nurses.

After working for a while doing hospice work, Ocie found it too draining, and, once again, quit nursing. Heading back up to San Francisco, she found herself working, this time as a nurse for the San Francisco Jail System.

> I feel I completed another mission that I didn't know I had, and that was touching the lives of young Black youth who were in jail for all sorts of stuff. I found myself compassionate, wanting to be there. And I ended up raising a whole lot of youth in that jail system. Actually, some of them were calling me "Mama," because I'd sit them down and bless them out good about what they needed to do to turn their lives around.

While working in the jail, Ocie also got very involved in educating the women on how to prevent pregnancy. She hated that many of the women were resorting to abortions, and was determined to teach them more effective types of birth control. Nursing in the jails turned out to be the most satisfying work Ocie had ever done.

After a six-year stay with the jails in San Francisco, Ocie returned to the desert, and dabbled in private nursing. She's still on call to fill in as a school nurse when they need a substitute.

Ocie had also embraced a new religion, Buddhism. She had studied a number of different religious philosophies before finding the one that felt right to her. A Japanese woman had invited her to a meeting and when they got there, people were chanting.

The minute I heard it, I knelt down, I looked around, they were chanting. It just did something. It felt good.

I've found more peace of mind and peace inside with myself than I ever had known. I have such peace within. And I can find it, I can get it when I want it. When something troubles me, I know I can get it with this process.… It's given me everything I need.

I could pray with my friends, and pray with others. And nobody is bothering me. I mean, nobody is trying to crucify me for that. Nobody is trying to lay guilt on me, telling me I'm going to hell because I'm a lesbian. It's a good feeling. It's a great feeling.

I went through a whole lot of changes about my life. I went through a whole lot of guilt about feeling those ideas [loving women], and I ran from it for a long time. But I think the best way I can put this… is to say it took me a long time to realize that there's nothing wrong with what I feel. There's nothing wrong with loving a woman.

Ocie continues to live in Arizona.
Interviewer: Arden Eversmeyer

Betty Rudnick

Born December 1924 in Texas
Interviewed in 1998 at age 74

And, you can't forget the uniforms!

Not many women can say they had an FBI agent assigned to watch them for more than a decade, simply because they loaned an acquaintance $100. But then everyone who knew Betty Rudnick would have quickly told you she was not just any woman!

Betty grew up in Houston, Texas, part of a working-class Jewish family. Early on she learned: "How you are going to get out of the social class you are in and into another class is education. ... Boys became doctors ... but girls were different. Girls were supposed to marry doctors."

Graduating in 1941, at 16 years old, Betty took some business classes and began working in Washington, D.C., as a clerk. It wasn't long before she knew that wasn't what she wanted. She tried to join the Army, but was turned down because she wasn't yet 18. Then Betty found out about a newly forming Cadet Nurse Corps. "Girls who went to nursing school could go for free. And then they could go into the Army. ... I had no interest in nursing whatsoever, but I wanted to be in the Army." Betty had really wanted to be a lawyer.

> *But, number one, women weren't being that readily admitted to schools of law. And number two, there wasn't any money. ... I could get my [nursing] education paid for, and it was a way to make a living. And, you can't forget the uniforms!*
>
> *Mine had a little Montgomery tam with some piping, a particular cross on it, an overcoat, and a gray suit. ... We got a cape, which was blue wool on the outside and red wool on the inside, which you could put on and throw over your shoulder!*

Studying nursing didn't thrill her, but Betty's attraction to uniforms and the camaraderie with other students kept her interested.

Betty had dated a young man who had gone off to war, and when he returned, they married. "Very quickly after that happened, I had the suspicion that it had been a mistake." When he took a job in Lake Charles, Louisiana, Betty quit school to go with him. Her husband was underemployed, and Betty was bored. Restless, she talked him into letting her move back to Galveston so she could finish her nurse's training. Meanwhile, he went to visit his family in West Texas.

Betty was working in Galveston, in the operating room, when she was summoned to take an urgent phone call. Her husband had impulsively bought into a linen shop and wanted her to quit nursing school again, and join him in West Texas. Her earlier

Betty in 1944

suspicions, that she'd made a mistake by marrying, were now confirmed. She told her husband it was over and to get a divorce.

Once Betty had graduated, she moved back to Houston, and went to work at a hospital. World War II was winding down and the Nurse Corps was being demobilized, so Betty didn't get to join and wear the uniform after all.

"It was during that time that I met this woman." She and her girlfriend, Sammie, had been together about five or six years, when Sammie suddenly married a man who'd been one of her patients. Betty was shaken.

> I went to a psychiatrist. I decided this was not any kind of life. It was obviously unacceptable. If a person had ambition, they were not going to get any place with this lifestyle [lesbianism]. The psychiatrist said, "What did you plan to do instead?" I recall that question and I said, "Well, there aren't too many options, are there? You can be celibate, or you can [get married]." So at that point, for a time, I dated men.
>
> At one point, I thought I was pregnant, and I got married again. However, I wasn't, and I got unmarried pretty quick!

Her varied experiences working in nursing made it clear to Betty that she wanted something more, so she began taking higher level classes, amassing 120 credits before she knew it. Since it wasn't possible to get a master's degree in nursing in Texas at that time, Betty moved to New York, and enrolled at Columbia University to pursue her goal.

Betty tested for admittance to the doctoral program as soon as she had her master's degree in hand. She'd done extremely well on almost all of the test, but she was slow on the reading part, and wasn't admitted. Betty headed back to Houston, and had barely returned and taken a job, when she got a letter inviting her to come back to Columbia to study for her Ph.D.

"I had met this woman who was a night supervisor [at the hospital in Texas]. And so I asked her [Cass] if she wanted to ride along. And one thing led to another." Cass and Betty lived together in New York for several years, Betty working toward her doctorate, and Cass working toward her master's at separate schools. Cass began to drink. "It wasn't all that much fun, but we went ahead. Then she dropped out, and went back to Galveston ... and I stayed in New York."

As soon as she'd completed her studies in New York, Betty went back to Texas again, making her the first woman in the state with a doctorate in nursing. She also became the youngest dean of a major school in the United States, when she became part of the faculty at the School of Nursing in Galveston, where she had started her nursing career.

Betty reconnected with Cass in Galveston, and they rekindled their relationship. Cass taught at the same school as Betty, and was unhappy when Betty rose in the ranks to Assistant Dean, and then even higher, to Dean of the School of Nursing. Cass's resentment and ongoing alcohol issues strained their relationship.

"I didn't have much knowledge about alcoholism at that point, or what to do about it. That was a real problem." Cass resented it when Betty couldn't invite her to socialize with her co-workers, so Betty suggested Cass go back to New York to finish her master's. They tried again later, but drinking was still a big issue, and their relationship failed.

It was during this time in her career that President Lyndon Baines Johnson asked Betty to serve as Assistant Surgeon General of the United States. Betty refused, but only after she held out long enough that Johnson had asked her himself!

Working in nursing administration in Texas at that time presented all sorts of dilemmas, not the least of which was all the politics. That aspect of her job eventually became too much for her. After fighting for years to make sure her programs were properly structured and funded, Betty decided it just wasn't worth it and resigned. Fortunately, she'd made lots of good connections, and it wasn't long before Betty was the Assistant Dean for Medical Surgical Nursing at the University of Kentucky.

Betty again became involved with another woman in uniform, a commander in the Nurse Corps. Her new girlfriend had been raised Southern Baptist, but when she joined the Navy, the woman converted to Catholicism. "Every time she had a relationship with a woman, she would then decide that Easter or Christmas was coming on, and she worried that she might die outside a state of grace. So she would then go to confession and communion until the next woman came along." The commander's personal conflicts soon became too much, and they parted ways.

Betty next met Gretchen, who had two children, and they lived together as a family for several years. Betty knew she didn't relate well to kids, but after her relationship with Gretchen was over, she became involved with Linda, who, just like Gretchen, had two children still at home.

"I was never good with these children. The notion that you would keep repeating the same pattern, and there is some purpose in it, I reject that whole notion. It was just an accident. It just happened that way." The relationship lasted a few years before Betty decided to let it go.

During her working years, Betty was never out. In Betty's own estimation, avoiding coming out to anyone was "just probably from basic cowardice." Like most of the women of her times, Betty never really came out to her family either.

> *Through the years, I brought my lover of the time to the family, to various holidays, to various dinners. … Since we're talking about over a period of years and several women, different women, Jennie [her sister] had to know [about me]. That was just making it easy on myself, I'm sure.*

While working in Kentucky in the early 1970s, Betty became involved in various women's groups, helped form a rape crisis center, taught a course on women and alcohol, and lent her house and yard to be used for a class on self-defense. One day, one of the young women Betty knew through her involvement in these programs, called to ask her a favor. She had been a student at Brandeis, and was now working at a local health food store.

The young woman said her mother was sick, and she needed to borrow $100. "I'll write you a check," Betty offered. "No, I can't really use a check. I need cash." The young woman told her up front that she might not ever get it back, and Betty gave her the money anyway.

Weeks later when *Time* magazine ran an article featuring the

FBI's Ten Most Wanted list, Betty realized the young woman she had helped was on that list. She had been a radical activist, and was wanted for her involvement in a bank robbery in which a guard was killed.

It wasn't long before the FBI came knocking on Betty's door. Since she had feared something like this might happen, Betty had already consulted a friend with the Attorney General's Office, who had advised her. She was not obligated to answer the FBI's questions, but any answers she did provide should be the truth. Betty was forthcoming with everything she knew.

"I had an agent of the FBI assigned to me from the time of the original [incident]." More than a decade later, when the space shuttle, Challenger, exploded in 1986, the FBI called Betty.

> I was then at Texas Women's University in Houston. And President Reagan was coming in to make a speech to the people at NASA, a kind of commemorative speech about the people who died. And they said to me, "What are you doing today?" I said, "Well, I had in mind to go to work and teach a couple of classes." And they said, "Well, we would like for you to go to work and for you to stay at the University until we call you and tell you that President Reagan has returned to Washington."… That was actually the last contact I had with them.

Betty wrapped up her career after working at several colleges in Texas. She had spent 42 years in nursing. For decades, she had been an unfailing advocate for nurses, demanding that the medical world recognize the essential role they played in health care.

Betty never felt secure enough to be out as a college administrator, but she did have to face a serious threat when, in 1977, someone reported that she had made physical advances to women students. The president of the University of Texas, Medical Branch, said, that because of this allegation, Betty could not be appointed as Dean of the School of Nursing at Texas Woman's University.

Betty knew the allegations weren't true, so she set out to find a good lawyer. The University had no evidence, and thus far hadn't fired her. And Betty hadn't lost any wages. That left the lawyer without much ammunition. Instead of trying to litigate, Betty went to the Board and asked them, "What kind of evidence did Dr. Truman Blocker offer you that this was so?" The president of the Board had to answer, "None." Confronted directly by Betty, the Board quickly backed down, and Betty became the dean.

Retirement afforded Betty the time to become more deeply involved with Hadassah, and with the Houston Area Women's Center Telephone Hotline for Battered Women. Both her mother and her sister had worked for decades with Hadassah, an organization of Zionist women. What interested Betty the most was their focus on raising funds to provide health care to children who had been abandoned during various wars. She also helped form, and was a mainstay in, LOAF, a social and support organization for mid-life and old lesbians in the Houston area.

Best yet, retirement gave Betty more time to sit out at the end of the pier fishing, talking, and laughing with her friends.

Betty died in January 2000.
Interviewer: Arden Eversmeyer

At age 74, with Ruddy

Emma Lou 'Scottie' Scott

Born in 1934 in Texas
Interviewed in 2007 at age 70

We lived happily ever after.

Scottie can legitimately say that the path her life would take was determined by an illness. She had grown up in a household with little or nothing. Her father, a drinker and carouser, left the family when the kids were young. So Scottie's mother rode two buses to work daily, and took in a renter to make ends meet.

By the time she was in high school, athletics were Scottie's life. Surrounded by fellow students taking part in many of the same sports, it didn't take long for Scottie to figure out that there were other girls who were "just like her." She dated a bit, "all the time knowing that there was, you know… I liked women more than men." When the man she was dating asked her to marry him, she turned him down, saying she wanted to "get established in her profession first."

Two of her running buddies in school were Helen and June.

Helen called me. That's when we'd just barely got a telephone. I guess she suspected that I might be gay. She and June were together, but then Helen sort of pursued me. So, Helen, I guess, was the one that indoctrinated me, brought me out.

In 1952, that pivotal moment occurred. Scottie began to have health problems in the middle of her high school years, unexplainable swelling and weight gain.

Mother would take me to the doctor, and they said, "Oh, she's just allergic to strawberries." Of course we didn't even have strawberries! Or [they'd say] tomatoes or something. Just allergic to something.

Well, then we went on a hayride … and I really got sick. I couldn't sleep laying down. I had to sleep sitting up. I went to school, and I couldn't bend my legs or arms … to get down to my locker or anything.

Finally, after taking me to many other doctors, Mother and I went to Ripley House [in Houston], where they had the doctors that were coming there for the clinic. They evidently took the urine specimen, and called my mother in and said to me, "You're about that far [holding their fingers about a half inch apart] from being dead. And if you don't do what I say to do, you'll never play sports again."

That certainly got Scottie's attention. She spent several weeks in the hospital being treated for severe nephritis (inflammation of the kidneys) and several more weeks recovering. Missing so much school kept Scottie

Scottie (center) with her siblings

from graduating with her class, and kept her from some of her sports... but not all! "I still couldn't participate in too many sports, but the last part of the semester I could.... So I got to be on the volleyball team, and I played archery. I got an archery letter and a volleyball letter. And a softball letter."

That fall, Scottie headed off to college. "My physical education teacher, Juanita Donophan, got me a $100 scholarship... to Sam Houston State Teachers College."

I majored in Health, Physical Education, and Recreation—and it wasn't at that time called dance, but we did have dance. The good old modern dance with the leotards that we had to put on!

June and Helen had gone off to TWU [Texas Women's University] and I went to Sam Houston State Teachers College. I was still talking to them. Helen and June broke up, so then that summer June and I got together.... At the same time, I was playing some ball in the summer, playing with one of the banks.

Fast pitch softball was a huge sport in Texas at that time, and many businesses sponsored teams. While not all the women involved were lesbians, many were. So was a big part of their fan base. Playing softball was where Scottie first met Arden Eversmeyer, who would later develop the Herstory Project.

"I took every class I could in physical education. We didn't have any competition with any other school, except with badminton." They didn't travel far, but Scottie and her teammates did get to play against women at other colleges. "We'd dress up and go like we were a professional team, so to speak."

After working a summer job following college graduation, Scottie took her first teaching position at Pershing Junior High.

It was a very big learning experience! We had five teachers. We all had 70 in every class! We had outside activities a lot. We cut the lines in the grass for the volleyball court. We cut the lines in the grass for softball. And then we also taught... I taught four periods of folk dance, and two periods of modern dance, for six weeks per semester to the ninth graders for seven years. There went my feet!

Scottie and June had been on again, off again through most of their college years. At one point, Scottie got the proverbial "Dear Jane" letter from June. When they ran into each other at a New Year's Eve party several years after they'd graduated, they reconnected once again. "We moved in together in 1960. Then, after we had lived together for two or three years, she up and left me."

During that era, junior high physical education teachers were also expected to serve as referees on their own time. But Scottie wanted more from her career, and started taking more college courses. "I drove to Sam Houston State Teacher's College and back … to work on my master's degree. I had no partner at that time because we were teaching 300 kids a day, plus [I was] going to Sam Houston."

Working and going to school was as much as Scottie could manage. As she put it, there was "no time for courting." So she and a friend, Patsy, decided to "batch it," sharing a house.

Living in a house enabled Scottie to get her first Scottie … her first Scottish terrier, that is. And she got her first camper. "I had a little 15-footer with no potty."

Scottie's persistent personality paid off when she earned her master's degree and got a better job. This time, she was teaching at Sam Houston High School, the oldest existing high school in Texas. Lyndon B. Johnson had taught there.

I went there to be the swimming coach, but they never would put in the heater in the swimming pool. So I could never get anybody to go swimming. I tried it a couple of years, and I kept the swimming team going. But then I became the volleyball coach.

So I coached them for the rest of my years with volleyball. At some point, I had the track team for a year or two; then I had the tennis team for 15 years. So all of that time, it was work, work, work.

It wasn't really all work and no play, though. Around 1965, Scottie met Janice. She'd first been introduced to Janice while she was still working toward her master's degree, and a few years later they met again. Going to a birthday party at Janice's house, Scottie took a gift. "I took her a little blue vase that we still have to this day."

As Scottie's current relationship broke up, she'd heard Janice's had too, and decided to go visiting.

> *I got in the car and I was driving to go see Janice, and see what she was doing, you know. She was probably lonely, and I was lonely. My stomach was upset, so I stopped at a drug store. … I went in, and Janice was standing there. So if I hadn't of stopped for my Titralac that night, and gone on to her apartment and she wasn't there, I probably wouldn't have stopped. But then I went on to her apartment, and we talked a long time that night.*

A week or so later, Scottie and her friends helped Janice move from her apartment to Scottie's house.

> *Janice had her own room at that time, so we weren't really together. I was in my bedroom, she was in her bedroom. But one morning Janice decided she's going to kiss me before she left. … So then Janice and I got together.*

Making the relationship work was an ongoing issue. They bought their first house, where they lived for five years, and later bought a second house, where they have lived for 36 years. Janice worked for the US Post Office as a mail carrier—or as they laughingly say, she was their neighborhood's finest streetwalker.

> *She got home at 3 or 3:30 [in the afternoon]. I didn't come home 'til 7:30, 8:30, 9:30 or 10 because of volleyball games; or volleyball refereeing if I wasn't coaching. … So we were never at home in the evenings. Her days off were always either Friday, Saturday, or Sunday, and I couldn't be off on Friday and Saturday because I had volleyball games.*

Like many other lesbians living in Texas during those times, Scottie and Janice never felt safe coming out to anyone other than their close friends. In the '80s, when more and more women were coming out, Scottie and Janice carefully tested the waters by going to Just Marion & Lynns, a local women's bar. "The bar had a garage door that went up. And about the first time I was there, here comes one of my students, so we slipped out underneath the doors."

Scottie felt sure her family knew she was a lesbian, but she never came directly out to them.

> *I'm sure my sister knew, because I suspect that my sister might have been in a "relationship" until she met her husband. She was with a lady named Helen, and they did everything together. They went to Mexico together. They went to California together. For five years, I think they had a ... may have had a "close relationship." Now, whether or not it was a sexual relationship, I don't know.*
>
> *My mother knew that I lived with women all of those years.... When you see pictures of my mother back when she was 21 or 22, in big high boots and what they called "military*

The apple doesn't fall far from the tree: Scottie's mom in the center

pants," Aunt Flora and her both—you think, "Okay, you just look really dykey right there!"

But as far as ever telling Mother, or my sister, or my brother... To say, "Brother, I'm a lesbian." No. To say it to my sister, never.

Scottie and Janice's love of camping, and campers, took them on all sorts of adventures. They managed to camp in every state, upgrading their campers every so often. They also became involved in RVing Women.

After teaching at the same school for 26 years, Scottie retired in 1990. It was a beginning, rather than an end. First she became involved in LHI, the Lesbian Health Initiative, a Houston organization focusing on lesbians, that gives free mammograms. It was a cause dear to her heart, in part because of her own experiences—she'd had ten operations for cystic breasts. Scottie had also lost her sister, at age 59, to breast cancer. And involvement in LHI hasn't just meant donating a few hours, or a few dollars. Scottie gives generously of her time, helping to obtain grants, and serving on their board.

She's also been active in LOAF, Lesbians Over Age Fifty, since its inception 20 years ago. "I keep dreaming that I would win the lottery... I could give a lot of it to LOAF and LHI." Of course, she'd also want to give some of her new-found fortune to the Texas Rambling Roses, her local RV Women's group.

Exemplifying the adage about being busier once you retire than you ever were when you worked full time, Scottie is also very involved in AssistHers, a group that gives help to lesbians with all types of disabilities. She's also involved in Angel Flight, volunteers who provide transportation for cancer patients and their loved ones flying in and out of Houston to go to MD Anderson (a world renowned cancer hospital/research institution in Houston).

The list could go on. Scottie is one busy, busy woman! And her activities aren't limited to volunteer work with organizations. The jock in her still demands attention on a regular basis. Scottie is very competitive in several sports, but her true talent is in badminton.

Article about Scottie and her sister in the Houston newspaper

The Senior Games, I've been involved in them since I was 55. ... The Gay Games, and Senior Games. They have all kinds of different activities ... I did the shotput, discus, and javelin. You have to qualify in your local, and then you have to qualify in your state, before you can go to the nationals. ... My first badminton nationals was in Tucson, where we won singles and fourth (bronze medal) in doubles.

In '06, I got to go to the Gay Games. ... I flew [to Chicago] by myself, with my badminton racquet. ... I played with a guy who was 40 something. And here I am, 70! He was my mixed doubles partner. We played for four days, and I won a bronze medal in singles in my age group, which was 70 to 74. ... I played with a young girl who was probably only 25 in lady's doubles, because we didn't have to play by age, and we won a bronze medal.

In 2007, Scottie received a special honor when she was inducted into the Texas Seniors Hall of Fame. She modestly offers, "I had what the qualifications were; I had about 300 medals in local and state. The gold, two silver and two bronze medals in badminton nationals was sort of what got me in." The list of sports in which she earned a medal in the Senior Games includes: table tennis, swimming (the backstroke), 3 on 3 basketball, archery, long jump, bowling, soccer, pickleball, cycling... and that's just a small sampling!

Almost 46 years with Janice, her continued involvement in assorted sports, her volunteer work for a wide array of causes, as well as raising Sadie Sue, a new puppy (and her fifth Scottie dog), have all contributed to Scottie's one-line description of her life.

"We lived happily ever after."

Scottie, Janice and Sadie Sue continue to thrive in Texas.
Interviewer: Arden Eversmeyer

Author's note from Margaret: Talk about a small world! In the fall of 2006, a young woman doing some work for me in Washington state noticed a photo I had on my desk. I had been working on a newsletter article for OLOC that featured Scottie. Pointing and stammering, the young (30-ish) woman declared, "That's the woman who beat the pants off of me at the Games in Chicago a couple of weeks ago!"

Betty
Shoemaker

Born July 1918 in New Jersey
Interviewed in 2001 at age 83

But you don't know what it's like to be 82.

"It was up and down." That's what Betty casually says about her life.
She was born in an era when flu epidemics killed so many people
that coffins stayed stacked on the streets for days because they
couldn't bury them fast enough. Betty lost her mother when she was
three months old, and her father a year later. She'd had pneumonia
along with her mother, and the doctor told her family "Don't bother
with the baby — she's not going to live anyway." Her grandmother
ignored their advice, and nursed Betty back to health.

Betty and her older sister were raised by her mother's family,
who provided a home and education, along with "a great deal of
physical abuse." She and her family experienced the Depression
living on welfare, depending on gifts of food and wearing second-
hand clothes.

Given the way their lives had started, it wasn't surprising that
Betty was almost inseparable from her sister as they went through

school. Her sister was the brilliant one. Betty was the popular one, always fooling around in school. "I enjoyed playing, especially when I was away from home, because you couldn't play when you were at home. It was strictly banned."

Before Betty even started high school, she knew she was different. "Everybody was getting interested in boys and I thought they were silly." While still in high school, Betty made friends with a woman from her neighborhood who was an English teacher. "I would go over there, and we would read poetry at night. The house was still lit by gaslight, so it was very romantic for a young girl." The teacher became Betty's first sexual experience.

In her sophomore year of high school, Betty almost ruined her relationship with her sister by having an affair with the female senior class president. Her sister was mortified. Laughing, Betty said, "I was tall … I could act and I had this neat voice, so I was a hero in a lot of the plays. And I had little girls writing me poetry, and that sort of thing. … and I could lead in dances." Others may have hated their high school experience, but Betty loved it, especially since life at home was so restrictive.

Betty went to work as a telephone operator as soon as she was out of high school, working from 4 p.m. to midnight, 6 nights a week for $14 a week. That was about 30¢ an hour. "Nobody in these days would believe anything like that, but that's true!"

All her co-workers were women, and they were required to wear gloves and have their skirts a certain length. "You couldn't speak to either of the operators beside you. You had to stay focused." After two years, Betty was trained to be a supervisor, but she was worried that her co-workers already resented her since she'd taken Latin, French, and chemistry in high school. And she didn't care for the "whole business of being a fink."

During her time as a telephone operator, Betty became enamored of a Quaker woman, and began attending meetings just to be near her. As things become more strained at home, Betty moved in with the 49-year-old woman, and stayed with her for six years. Then she quit the phone company and drove a cab three years, making good money from tips.

Chatting with one cab fare about her desire to go on to

college resulted in her getting a scholarship that sent her to Temple University in Philadelphia. The fare turned out to be a state senator.

After finishing her four-year degree, Betty opted to attend a summer program at Wellesley. "That summer, five men wanted to marry me! And they were all really interesting men, with money and all the rest of that stuff. And..." Betty paused for dramatic effect. "I married a homosexual!" Laughing, Betty tells that they knew about each other, but thought together they could lead a straight life. Her husband soon "started having deviations with men again." When they separated, Betty went out to sow her own wild oats.

Betty at 27

That was my real straight period. I had [as] many love affairs with men as most men have with women. And good sex with some, but [I] never found the emotional depth that I found in women.

Serving cocktails at a jazz club kept Betty busy that year. While she was working at the club, Betty became involved with one of the patrons, and became pregnant. Realizing the father was so immature she would have been raising two children (him and the baby), she made the difficult choice to raise her child alone, something very few women intentionally did at that time.

Betty took a job cleaning at a nearby school so she could keep her daughter, Star, with her, but her daughter's chronic lung problems motivated Betty to move to a drier climate. She and Star settled in Santa Fe, New Mexico.

It was a wonderful time in my life ... because I had tremendous lovers there, and my daughter did well in school and all. ... I met Ann, the woman that I had the really passionate love affair of my life with, and we were together for seven years.

But Ann's drinking became a problem, and to deal with it, Betty began drinking. "It was so destructive to our relationship ... and we finally split up."

On the rebound, Betty entered into another relationship that lasted about five years. "She was a very brilliant woman, but she was a paranoid schizophrenic ... those were hard times." Betty and her daughter were now living in California; the teenaged Star was beginning to have problems with depression.

When Betty had had all she could take of her current relationship, she broke up with the woman, who subsequently killed herself. In retrospect, Betty feels this experience gave her daughter the idea that suicide would be the answer to her own problems. Star attempted suicide numerous times over the following decade or so.

Her ex-partner's death, and her daughter's struggles, helped motivate Betty to get sober. It took three attempts, but with the help of a residential program, Betty succeeded.

Betty then worked for nine years as an administrator in California, where she felt she was being harassed by another employee. She was suddenly fired two days before Christmas. Now 58 years old, Betty felt her only recourse was to try for unemployment compensation, but her daughter's lover offered to help her get a lawyer and pursue it legally. Once in court, the opposition brought up the fact that she was a lesbian, and started talking about Betty's alleged unwanted attention to a female co-worker.

"I was fortunate enough to get a woman judge, and I believe she was a lesbian." Betty was relieved when the judge called the opposing lawyer over and said, "I don't want this woman's sex life dragged all over this courtroom — go outside and settle on her terms." And, as Betty put it, "they paid me handsome!" In addition to a cash settlement, the hospital had to continue to support her until she became eligible for Social Security.

Life took an even more difficult turn as Betty approached age 60. Her daughter, Star, finally succeeded in committing suicide. It almost pushed Betty back to drinking. "If I was ever going to drink, it would have been then. But I got through it. I was almost going to [drink], and then I thought 'No, I'm not going to desecrate her memory by doing that.'"

This time of her life also brought about a move from San Francisco to Santa Monica, where she lived on the money the hospital was providing. There she started a group for old lesbians, and connected with the next love-of-her-life, Sylvia. They provided temporary housing for lesbians moving into the area, and sponsored a series of dances and art shows. Their efforts evolved into a unofficial women's center. "We had a conference for older lesbians there. I mean we didn't call it that, but that's what it was."

Together, they traveled to the British Isles. Betty also started a small women's bookstore, but when Sylvia became ill she gave the store up to help take care of her. They were together 12 years when Sylvia died.

Betty was once again looking for community after Sylvia's death. She'd heard there were plans to create a conference specifically for old lesbians, and got involved. This led to her serving for several years on the steering committee for OLOC during it's development.

Passing the 70 year mark barely slowed Betty down, as she traveled repeatedly to Provincetown to attend several Golden Threads events. (Golden Threads is a contact organization for lesbians of all ages, but mosty older women. For years, it also held annual conferences.) On her second trip, Betty "met a very exciting and interesting woman, and had a love affair with her." And when that didn't work out, Betty was still not done. She met Vashtee, and started yet another involvement, a relationship that still brought her joy as she told her story at age 83!

Vashtee and Betty in 2000

Late in her life, Betty had a conversation with her sister, who had only had one sexual partner her whole life. Debating whether or not that was a good thing or a bad thing, Betty allowed that she didn't equate sex and morality.

> *Morality to me is not being an imbecile. Or telling lies. But nothing to do with sex.*
>
> *I've never been traditional in the way I live. I've always been sort of on the edge, in a certain sense of the word. So when people say "Oh yeah, I know how you must feel." I tell them "you know what it was like to be 30, 'cause you've been 30 before. But you don't know what it's like to be 82."*

Betty died in 2002.
Interviewer: Arden Eversmeyer

Ruth Silver

Born March 1919 in New York
Interviewed in 2001 at age 82

I'm saving the best for last.

Few children grow up aware that, without doubt, they were neither planned for, wanted, or needed in their family. This was Ruth's inauspicious beginning. Although her parents were both physically present in her early life in Brooklyn, Ruth was essentially raised by a sister, nine years her senior, sharing her bed and tagging along everywhere she went. A reading disability presented Ruth with some unique challenges that she met by being able to memorize almost anything she heard.

Ruth was a math whiz, bored with school by the time she was ten. She became a fixture on the street corner, where she concentrated on honing her yo-yo skills to such a high level that the Brooklyn Daily Eagle once ran an article, with photos, when she won the Brooklyn Yo-Yo Championship. Unfortunately, at least from Ruth's point of view, truant officers put an end to her fledgling yo-yo career. They sent her back to school. She had fallen so far behind, that she was held back a year, and now it was even harder for Ruth to fit in. She was traumatized by being behind all her friends in school.

"I was different than all the others. In many ways, I knew that I wasn't a girlie-girl. I knew that I wasn't good enough ... to go on with them to the next grade." Ruth turned to her love of athletics to get her through.

When she finally made it to sixth grade, like many other young women, she developed a crush on her gym teacher, Miss Scanlon. But it felt like it was more than a crush to Ruth.

Miss Scanlon figured out that Ruth couldn't read, and involved her in a project teaching first graders phonics, knowing that in the process Ruth would also learn to read. She also earned 25¢ a week helping her teacher with chores, and demonstrating gymnastic skills to other students. Ruth had earned $12.50 by the end of the year, half of what it would cost her to spend the summer at a camp in upstate New York. She was surprised when her parents matched her earnings, and 13 year old Ruth went off to the country where, in her family's words, "she would learn all kinds of things." And learn she did.

I discovered who I was at that time. I mean, there was no question. I knew that I was different, but I had found people like myself. I found other "lesbians". ... I finally found my place in the world.

Ruth was still too young to officially become a part of the camp staff, but she found her niche teaching dancing and crafts, and returned the second summer as a counselor-in-training. Back home during the school year, Ruth's grades improved, and she was able to move on to high school.

Thinking there was no way she'd ever get into college, Ruth entered a high school that focused on the arts. She had struggle to prove herself, and she showed everyone up by taking both algebra and geometry in one semester, scoring 100% when tested, and winning medals for being the best runner. Ruth had also begun working at the local community center, teaching many of the same classes she had taught at camp. Despite already earning more by teaching individual classes than a social worker did, Ruth began to look into the requirements for that field. She was discouraged when she learned classes at her art-centered high school wouldn't get her into college.

A junior in high school and 15 years old, Ruth dropped out to work full time and, with lots of drama and trauma, moved out of the family home. After all, as her mother reminded her at the top of her lungs, "Jewish girls never left their home until they were married."

Ruth's religious upbringing had been full of contradictions, at best. "We were essentially cultural Jews and atheists, believing not in a God, but in the goodness of people." Ruth had attended Shul (Jewish school) to learn Yiddish, Jewish culture, and history, but not religion.

Ruth embarked on a succession of jobs, while sharing an apartment with three friends from camp. Having dropped out of high school was gnawing at her. She found that she could go to college at night as a "non-matriculated student," but she wouldn't be awarded the college credits until she finished high school. Continuing to work full time, Ruth began taking night college courses and, at the same time, attending night high school.

Reading was still a problem. "I worried about every class I was taking ... and how much reading I was going to have to do." Not to let her reading difficulties slow her down, Ruth says she "was fortunate in getting some of my lovers to read for me."

After getting her high school diploma, Ruth was able to focus on the classes that would lead to a career in social work. Oddly enough, that included gym classes. At that time, to get into the social work school at New York University, you had to be a physical education major.

Ruth's natural athletic abilities gave her the options of playing soccer, basketball, or field hockey. All of the coaches wanted her. But her outside activities, a full time job and "making and selling stuff," was earning so much money that she didn't want to give it up. It was hard for her to focus on staying in school. Fascinated by silver working and weaving, Ruth managed to get a scholarship to take classes, so she could add new skills to her ever growing repertoire. She quickly mastered silver working, and was hired to train men at a costume jewelry shop for $42 a week, a princely sum for the 1930s. She was soon designing her own jewelry pieces, many of which went into mass production.

Notwithstanding her young age (16) and college class load, Ruth took on another project, working with a pilot program for children at the National Association of Manufacturers. She helped develop a company, Gemcraft, which crafted jewelry from a brand new material called "plastic." And her new skills led Ruth to a position making three dimensional plastic models of nail polish and lipstick cases for a new startup business...Revlon!

Never one to stay still, Ruth found herself mesmerized by a display of custom leather goods displayed in a window she passed on her way to school. She called on sewing skills she'd developed at an early age, when her mother had told her "nayzich alaine," which translated into "sew it yourself." Ruth took a job working at the leather shop keeping their sewing machines running. And, of course, she couldn't help but learn about working with leather, which led again to her designing pieces of her own.

"I was earning very good money," Ruth recalls. She had become the floor manager at the store in New York. When the company set up a manufacturing facility in Pennsylvania, Ruth took the opportunity to start a new adventure, leaving behind a faltering relationship with her current lover. Ruth hired and trained staff to produce leather goods in larger quantities sold across the country in such stores as Neiman Marcus and Hartzfeld. She was treated like a queen by the leather company, which paid her rent in both New York and Pennsylvania, and bought her tickets on the train to commute each week.

The company decided to buy Ruth a car to save money, and took her out to an old mine to learn how to drive in one day. Two days later, she took the driving test. She drove into New York City the next day. Unfortunately, once Ruth had their manufacturing staff hired and trained, the company began to renege on promises they had made. Ruth decided to leave, and embarked on her own leather enterprise back in New York.

At 27, Ruth opened a small shop of her own. She sold yarns

and knitting supplies in the front of the store, and produced her own custom leather goods in the back. Mary, Ruth's assistant in Pennsylvania, came to New York to join the new business venture. There were no apartments available, so they were invited to live with Ruth's parents. Ruth and Mary shared both their business and personal lives for four years. However, Mary wanted to have children, and a man, who had been pursuing her, pressed her to marry.

"You know I love you dearly. There's no way I can stand in your way, if it's what you really want," said Ruth. Mary got married, and Ruth grieved the relationship, and closed the store. Six months later she married a sweet, non-threatening guy from the neighborhood and had a baby.

Ruth and her husband moved to California and, as she says laughingly, she came out again ... this time as a straight woman! Still grieving her loss of Mary and her lesbian life, raising a baby, and struggling in her marriage, Ruth decided that she needed help. She turned to the study of massage for relaxation, but learned quickly that the body contact was too much for her.

Trying to come to terms with her earlier life with Mary, Ruth sought a Jungian therapist, who told her, "You have to get beyond it, and forget about that part of your life." Her therapist's single focus was to help Ruth "resolve" her lesbianism. To Ruth, that only meant she had to learn to keep her secrets better.

Taking the therapist's advice, Ruth focused on raising her two children (she now had a daughter and son), and working as a cooperative nursery school

Ruth at her wedding in 1950

Expressing her musical side in 1960

director. Later she utilized her many creative talents and human relations skills, working at a Jewish Community Center. It was during her 24 year tenure at the Center that Ruth remembers her first serious run-in with ageism. Applying for a full time position, she was told, "Well, you're fifty years old. You don't have a lot of time to put into this agency." The thirty-some-year-old Personnel Director quickly realized she'd made a big mistake by telling Ruth she was too old. "Lady, I've already given ten years of my life to this agency. Don't tell me I don't have time." Ruth got the new position, but vividly recalls her desire to "hit her [the Personnel Director] upside her head."

Through all her years at the Community Center, creating and running dozens of programs, Ruth kept her secret from everyone. In retrospect, Ruth feels that all the pressure contributed to her subsequent trial, facing breast cancer and a mastectomy. The brush with death changed Ruth's thinking about her life, and she adopted a new mantra, "I'm saving the best for last."

Her life at home had also experienced its own growing pains. "My husband and I lived almost separate lives. We would go to the theater together, do various things together, but we had no sexual relationship. We were like siblings in a household." By now, Ruth had acknowledged to herself that she was eventually going to leave the marriage. But as long as her job, and her life in the community were fulfilling, she stayed.

The women's movement was growing all around Ruth, and it challenged her status quo. She knew she was a feminist, but feared that involvement "would spell the end of my secure, false life." She didn't want to be left out altogether, so Ruth put her energies to organizing, starting women's study groups, and planning retreats.

Her safe, secure life was again shaken when her daughter, now in her 20s, came out as a lesbian. Ruth was haunted by the words of her therapist, who years ago had warned her, "If you don't resolve your lesbianism, it will be lived out in your daughter."

I was indeed a bad person. I hadn't done my work of totally ridding myself of my true nature, and of my love for women — and here was the result! My daughter was doomed to live out my unresolved experience.

At the same time, Ruth was excited that her daughter would have the chance to be true to herself, and not have to hide like she herself did. Her daughter's willingness to be open with her gave Ruth the courage to do the same.

"I broke my silence, and shared my former closeted life with my daughter. Just doing that much released me from some of my self-imposed bondage." But Ruth still hesitated to come out on her own, continuing to live her "straight life."

Tired of all the stress and politics of her job at the Community Center, Ruth retired at 64, wondering what was yet to come. Her creative streak took over again, and she became intrigued by hand quilting. She gathered a group of women friends who began meeting regularly to work on a quilt. Since they had to learn as they went along, the first quilt took almost a year to complete. Everyone immediately wanted to start another quilt, but Ruth was getting restless, wanting to move on to something more meaningful. She agreed to stay with the quilting group with one provision ... another quilt had to have some special significance.

After weeks of arguing over the focus of the project, Ruth's dormant feminism reared its head, and the group began work on a pieced quilt that paid tribute to American woman of historical importance. The quilters began by making up a wish list of women who should be included in the design. Making sure there was no duplication, each quilter chose a woman she admired and began making a panel. "After we finished the first ten, I said, 'Okay, now pick your second choice.'"

During the quilting project, Ruth attended the funeral of the mother of her best friend, Helen. At the funeral, Shevy, a childhood friend of Helen's, came over to ask Ruth what people do when they retire. Ruth invited Shevy to come to her house to see the quilt in progress.

Shevy had been in a film about six women in their sixties that had recently aired on public television. In the film, Shevy had openly shared that she had come out as a lesbian at age fifty. At Ruth's house, Shevy spoke up, saying, "You know, not one person said anything to me about being a lesbian." Surprisingly, it was Ruth's husband who responded first, saying, "Well, it's nobody's business. Who cares?" After offering some suggestions on what other women might be portrayed on the quilt, Shevy left.

Ruth and her family had acquired a house in the desert that they used as a retreat from the pressures of city life. Coincidentally, Shevy's home was not far from Ruth's retreat, and Shevy invited her to stop by next time she headed out to the desert. At their first visit, Ruth remembers opening the door and immediately saying, "You came out at fifty. I went in at thirty. What do you know?" To which Shevy responded, "It takes one to know one."

Quickly bonding, Ruth and Shevy spent weekends hiking and talking, and getting to know each other. "I fell, you know. I know why they call it 'falling in love.' We don't walk into love. We fall. I fell head over heels in love with that woman, and I said, 'She is not going to get away from me, period.'"

Embarking on the first of several adventures together, Ruth announced to her husband that she and Shevy planned to attend a four-week retreat at an Ashram in Massachusetts. When she returned home she told her

Ruth and Shevy in 1989

husband, "I've fallen in love with this woman. She's more than just simply a good friend. I'm in love with her." The decision was made to separate. Ruth decided she wanted to be the one to leave and put her things into storage.

Moving in together seemed like a logical step forward to Ruth, but it didn't materialize. She thinks Shevy felt safe being involved with a married woman, but wasn't ready to commit once Ruth left her husband. Shevy left the area, going back to the Ashram by herself. Ruth was devastated.

Ruth's sister had always been accepting of Ruth and Shevy's relationship, and encouraged her to work things out one way or the other. Ruth flew to see Shevy and was surprised when Shevy took her directly from the airport to a romantic weekend at a luxurious inn. Ruth and Shevy talked and agreed, they both wanted to give it a try. They spent a few months wrapping up their individual lives, and embarked on a new one together.

Talking things over with her estranged husband, Ruth asked, "Didn't you ever suspect?" He replied, "Women have always slept together. Why should I suspect anything?" He liked Shevy, and was happy for Ruth, and after 38 years of marriage they amicably divorced.

Gaining her son's acceptance wasn't as easy. When he found out Ruth was leaving to be with a woman, he said, "It was enough that I have to deal with my sister and her girlfriends." But when he realized the woman Ruth loved was Shevy, someone he already knew and liked, he conceded that it was okay after all.

At 69, Ruth had finally come back out, and started her new life. Ruth and Shevy dove headfirst into a life of activism, sharing their stories publicly, and helping to organize and empower other old lesbians to confront those "forces in our society which make it difficult for us to be ourselves."

Ruth helped finish the quilt. Each woman who participated added her own name along the edge. The completed quilt honored 42 women, and had a life of its own. It was used for the cover artwork of a catalog put out by the National Women's History Project, who then turned an image of the quilt into a poster that sold 20,000 copies.

One important outlet for Ruth and Shevy's collective activism was their involvement in forming and nurturing OLOC, an organization of lesbians 60 years and older. They were two of the founding members. They devoted considerable time and energy to finding other old lesbians, telling them about the newly formed organization that was exclusively for them.

Ruth and Shevy traveled all over the country in an RV for two years, enjoying the trip, the world around them and all of the opportunity to meet lesbians. At the end of their two years of travel, Ruth and Shevy settled in Apache Junction, Arizona, in one of the two predominantly women's RV resort parks.

They continued to fly here and there for speaking engagements. In their travels, they also fell in love with Discovery Bay Resort, an intentional community on the Olympic Peninsula in Washington. The two then split their time between the two sites, wintering in Arizona and summering in Washington.

Commenting about her life after coming back out of the closet and finding Shevy, Ruth says:

I have a new level of consciousness. The very idea that it is okay, or acceptable, to be a lesbian, to be old, and to live in this time is a joyous experience. It gives purpose to my life, that otherwise would have been a life of treading water and never getting to the other side. Now I feel that I am on the other side. I am proud to be old, to be a lesbian, to feel free to be myself.

Ruth lives in Arizona and Washington. Shevy Healey died in 2001. Interviewer: Arden Eversmeyer

At the age of 84, Ruth was wooed and fell in love again.

WOMEN'S HISTORY:
A PATCHWORK OF MANY LIVES

The "A Tribute to the American Woman" quilt consisted of 42 squares, each depicting an important American woman, including lesbians. A photo of the quilt was made into a poster (shown above) by the National Women's History Project, and was used as the cover for their 1992 national monograph. The quilt was later displayed in schools across the country.

Annalee Stewart

Born December 1927 in
Massachusetts
Interviewed in 2000 at age 73

What did you think I was going to do? Fire you?

Growing up presented interesting opportunities to Annalee. She
was the daughter of two Methodist ministers who were absolute
opposites of the religious right.

> *They were very much action-oriented, and very liberal, and I
> had a great, free childhood, especially compared to what I saw
> other preachers' kids have. They weren't very strict. I had a lot
> of conflict, but it was an internal kind of conflict, because I
> thought I was different from the other kids that I knew.*
>
> > *On some level, early on I knew I was different; I didn't
> know how to explain it. I remember in my childhood doing a
> lot of stuff with my brother, wanting to be a boy, thinking that
> my attraction to girls was like his. It was the only way I could
> explain it, and I had no words with which to talk about it. At
> one point I thought that it probably meant that I wanted to be a
> boy, or should have been a boy.*

As I look back on it in later years, I realize that it was an early awareness that that's where the power was; that my brother had the power in the family; that he could do things I wanted to do.

What Annalee wanted to do wasn't all that earthshaking. She simply wanted to hitchhike like he did.

I thought it was grossly unjust that I couldn't travel that way. I didn't understand what that was about. I dressed like my brother in the summer, and I cut my hair short. On some level, I was a little ashamed of it, or uncomfortable about it, when I got to the teen years. I wouldn't let anybody see those pictures, because I still couldn't explain this; I still felt a distance inside me that I couldn't account for.

I didn't know the word "lesbian" until I was fifty! But somewhere in there, during my adolescence, I fell in love with my best friend, Marilyn. I followed her around like a little puppy dog. She and I spent a lot of time together; we stayed at one another's house, since her mother was a working mother. I remember when she was ill, broke her foot and had her appendix removed, because with each, she came to my house to recuperate.

She and I thought that was wonderful, although I never told her anything about my feelings until we were

Fourteen year old tomboy

forty years old. But I followed her everywhere, and if Marilyn wanted me to do this or that, that was fine. … I knew that I had feelings for her, and I didn't understand what they were at that juncture. I just knew that they were not to be talked about. And I didn't know the words with which to talk about them.

Annalee first heard the word "homosexual" after she had started college. "You have feelings for somebody of the same sex. Now that began to sound like me." As she realized she also had crushes on other girls, things began to make a bit more sense to her. Annalee headed to the library to find out more but that process left her even more confused and frustrated.

Everything I read was written by males, generally by psychiatrists, about men who were very sick. I would read that, but I didn't understand some of the terms they referred to, and it didn't sound like anything I felt. I couldn't identify with it at all. So that left me out in the cold, knowing that it was same sex, but it was male, and I wasn't anything like these people.

I kept dating because that's what you were supposed to do, and besides, eventually some young man would kiss me, and the bells would go off like they did for Rock Hudson and Doris Day in some movie I had seen. I never got any bells.

She pushed her feelings aside and concentrated on her career. One very, very long year teaching fifth grade, then working office jobs for which Annalee felt totally unsuited, sent her back to school. This time she entered the seminary, thinking she'd follow in her mother's footsteps. "Got engaged there to a very nice young man. The bells kind of went off a little bit." But they broke up about a month before they were to be married. Looking back, Annalee knows he was gay, and that was part of what drew them together.

I still had this strong draw toward women, even while I was trying to date and get married, and all that. That still was very clearly an avenue of choice for me, in that I preferred being with my women friends, and I had more fun with them than with any date.

Age 23

Instead of finishing at the seminary, Annalee transferred to the University of Minnesota and got her master's degree in social work. Taking a job there, she roomed with a former classmate. When that classmate married and moved out, another friend of hers asked if Annalee was looking for a roommate.

We moved in, and we got to know more and more of each other and fell in love, and we were together twenty years!

It was funny because, even though we both were very close with one another, we continued just a little bit of dating. It was like, "Well, this is really only until Mr. Right comes along." We really hadn't given up that notion that we had been raised with: you know, gals get married. ... We're still good friends, and today we laugh at the dating we did.

We just knew we loved each other and we didn't have the word "lesbian" in our vocabulary. We had two sets of friends we hung around with a lot that we thought "might be like us." But we were all so closeted, we never would ask anybody, or raise any questions.

During that time, we both developed our careers, we each adopted a child, I ran for county commissioner in Dakota County (the first woman to run) and we were very public in a lot of ways. But nobody ever raised that question — out loud, at least. Because society was not acknowledging gay and lesbian people, we fell beautifully into that: "Oh, they live together because that gives them companionship and helps to share the expenses, and they're safer that way."

We were among the few women, at that time, who actually bought a house together. This was not common. The bank even hesitated to give us a second mortgage. We wanted to pick up the first mortgage because it was 5%, and they would not give us mortgage money. My father became so incensed that he borrowed money on his insurance. He loaned it to us.

My parents never asked about us, and it was never an open subject. We were single women living together. I was his daughter and wanted to do it. Therefore, those bankers should allow it. ... Our first check each month was written to Dad.

Most of Annalee's early career was spent as a County Probation Officer, and she was asked to be a supervisor in the state Corrections system. "It was the first time a woman supervised men. You would have thought the concrete was going to crumble!"

Even with leading what would appear on the outside to be an idyllic life, with kids (the children they had each adopted were from Korea), a good job, and a house, Annalee's settled routine was about to be shaken up. She and her partner's life together had been very closeted. But there was that piece of Annalee that could not sit quietly on the sidelines while social injustice was about to occur. It forced her to do some soul searching, and to take a stand. Unfortunately, her partner wasn't as ready to get involved in working for social change as Annalee was.

We were together for twenty years, and at the point that we broke up there was a campaign in St. Paul for human rights. Actually, gays and lesbians were included in the human rights ordinance. A Baptist minister started a campaign to have us removed ... I wanted to get involved, and several things had kind of come together for me.

I had gone to New Orleans to a conference. I thought I was far enough away from Minnesota that I could go to the gay caucus, and there would be no repercussions, so I went.

Annalee decided she would arrive at the meeting late, so she could slip in unnoticed, but everyone else was even later. She found herself alone, with her cup of coffee, until others got there.

I could see my group work teacher in graduate school referring to the social isolate, and using a diagram to make it clear. I got so tickled by it, that I picked up my cup and went down and joined them.

> *I met a woman from Rutgers University, a Puerto Rican woman who was very out. This was the first time I had met anybody my age, 50 years old, who called herself a lesbian and was out. I was like "Wow!" I followed her around all week-end, like a puppy dog, asking questions about this. I was like a sponge, I couldn't get enough. The whole weekend was total immersion.*

The impact of this new awakening was reinforced by other incidents. Annalee was now working full time as an instructor in the School of Social Work, at the University of Minnesota.

> *A student came to me and said, "I want to ask you something, and you don't need to answer if you don't want to." And I said, "Okay." And she said, "I was wondering, are you gay?" Well, nobody had asked me, and I hardly ever used "gay" or "gay/lesbian," but I really admired this student, and didn't feel comfortable lying. I told her that I hadn't told people, that I was just barely sticking my nose out of the closet, and when I did, it was in New Orleans, not Minneapolis.*
>
> *I told her how little I knew, so she and her partner had me over for dinner, and I went home with a stack of books that would choke an elephant! I read books, articles, listened to music, practically 24 hours a day, and just WOW! I found out there were coffee clubs. I didn't know they were there. There was so much I had no knowledge of, and it was like I couldn't get enough.*
>
> *The third thing that happened is that I knew I was going to have to go home and come out to my son, who was now in his senior year in high school. I was either going to have to tell him what was happening to me, or I was going to have to lie about where I was going. I didn't want him lying to me, so I didn't want to lie to him. I turned off the TV, and unplugged the telephone, and said that I needed to talk to him. And he responded as an adolescent would; he said, "What did I do?" I told him, "It isn't about you, it's about me."*

One of several times Annalee was arrested for practicing non-violent civil disobedience by taking part in a demonstration against the Honeywell Project in the early 1980s

I told him that everything I had taught him about responsibility, in terms of one's sexuality, was true, and that it was true for me as well. We all have to make decisions about our responsibility to ourselves and others, but that there was a major difference; that when I was his age, my attraction was to girls, not the opposite sex. And I told him that the first love I felt was for my friend Marilyn, whom he had known for many years. She'd been to our home and we'd been to hers, and he thinks she's really neat, so he could understand how a person could fall in love with her.

He took it very well. I didn't know what was going to happen. I told him that I was really scared to tell him, to which he responded, "What did you think I was going to do? Fire you?" I laughed. I didn't know. Actually, I was afraid he'd run away, or disown me.

Annalee began working on the campaign to protect lesbian and gay rights in Minnesota. Her parents had both been strong activists, so fighting for rights wasn't something new to her. She'd fought to integrate a playground that was set aside for whites only, when she was very young. She had been called "a communist." She had forcibly integrated a restaurant that would not serve black classmates, when she was in college. She had marched in protest of the Vietnam War. And she had been arrested several times protesting against Honeywell, a large manufacturer of cluster bombs.

Yet defending her own rights was a much scarier proposition. Annalee worried that someone might identify her as a lesbian.

I put on my polyester clothes and pearl earrings, which meant nobody was supposed to be able to tell that I was a lesbian. Everybody probably knew but me.

On one particular day, after I had talked with my son and was at the volunteer office, the TV press came and wanted to take pictures of the office. They had just come from the Baptist minister's group, and they wanted pictures from our group. They said, as they have always said, if anyone wants to go to the back room and not be in the pictures they could go, and it would be understood. So, I wrestled, because I wanted to go to the back room.

I thought of my son, being out and all this sort of stuff, but the other part of me was saying, "You didn't try to hide when you were demonstrating against Vietnam, or trying to open up the park or the restaurant or what have you. Here you have something that's probably the closest to your own personal experience, and you're thinking about hiding." I couldn't bring myself to do it; I couldn't go hide.

I sort of compromised with myself. I went to the farthest corner and turned my profile, and worked on the collator while they were taking the pictures. I stayed in the room with the idea that, of course, nobody would notice anything back in the corner. And then I thought, "Well, what am I going to tell my son?" I had said I'm not making a big splash out of this, and so I went home and told him about Channel 4 or 5 taking pictures, and that I couldn't leave the room. It just felt like a denial that I couldn't do.

I thought we should talk about it in case any of his friends, (I didn't think they watched the news that much) but in case they saw it, he should be prepared. We decided that if something came up, he could always say his mother was a social worker, and social workers believe that people should be able to live their lives the way they want to, as long as they are treating other human beings in respectful ways. So, he put two little TVs next to each other, and we watched them together in the living room, and there were pictures on both channels. He put his arm around me and said, "Mom, you're a TV star."

Eventually I came out [at the University]. I started teaching Ethno Cultural Concepts in Social Work Practice. It was a class to help students look at how they interact with people who are different from them. Of course, each of us is different, but this was specifically to look at racism, anti-Semitism, homophobia, and issues of disability. ... They worked in groups. ... There was always a group who chose gay/lesbian.

One day I went over to the Student Union and sat in on a movie in which this young Asian man talked about the whole issue of visibility and invisibility, and how this had played a part in his life in relation to his Asian ethnicity and his being gay. He could not hide being Asian; visually he was there. But he could hide being gay.

All of a sudden, it dawned on me that in my class, I was taking a "privilege" of invisibility … and I said to myself, "I can't do that anymore." I walked over to the classroom and came out.

LEFT TO RIGHT: MARGARET DOUSSETT, ANNALEE STEWART, MARTH BOESING, AND NANCY EDWARDS, 1996

THE WALKER ART CENTER PRESENTS
A TRIBUTE TO LESBIAN ELDERS
DYKE NITE VI

The sixth annual Dyke Nite celebrates elders with two nig! rollicking performances by artists of all ages paying tribut pioneers in the Twin Cities lesbian community. Emcees Pa

SATURDAY, JUNE 22
7 AND 9:15 PM
SUNDAY, JUNE 23, 7 PM
TICKETS $12 ($10)

Holman, Nancy Edwards, and Annalee Stewart welcome Simpatico, a jazz trio featuring Melissa Stout (flute). Ann Potter (vocals), and LaVern Christie (guitar): Buffalo Gals, bluegrass/country-western group; drummers Joanna Kad Cynthia Lane: dancer Etoy Wilson; and excerpts from the l lesbian soap opera *Toklas, MN.*

FOR RESERVATIONS: 375-7622 (TDD: 375-7585)

The evening also includes the premiere of *Voicing the Leg*

Annalee second from left.

Telling her class about her realization that she had the option of being invisible, while many of them did not, was very difficult, but in the end, liberating. "It was like shedding something. ... I kicked open the closet door forever!"

Annalee began routinely coming out to students. "I would announce at the first session that I was a lesbian, and I would tell them, 'I am telling you this because homophobia kept me in the closet for fifty years.'"

Annalee continued to be as out as possible in the larger community as well, and several years later traveled to be a part of the March on Washington.

> *It was tremendously exciting to go someplace and to know that the people around you are there for you. It was a beautiful experience. I felt safe. There is something about seeing thousands of people standing together to secure justice for themselves and others that makes you swell with pride.*

Retirement may have meant Annalee didn't go to work each day, but she certainly didn't stay home. Among other things, she has helped develop an LGBT alumni group at the University of Minnesota, and became involved in the leadership of OLOC.

She's also been involved in Dyke Night, a celebration held at a prestigious museum each summer. "This year they asked me if I wanted to be in the opening act, and I said, 'Oh, sure, if you want.'

Cheryl and Annalee in 2000   *With Marilyn in 2004*

I had no idea what it was going to be and it turned out to be a dance piece to the tune of "That's Entertainment." So I got to wear my tuxedo, with all the trimmings!"

Annalee has had several very important women in her life: Joyce, Betty, Pat and Cheryl, as partners, and many others through long years of friendship.

> On my 70th birthday, I had a huge birthday party.... Marilyn flew out from the East Coast. She, and each of my partners, were introduced with my tribute and thanks to them, as the women who have influenced my life and contributed to my growth and happiness...and, of course, sometimes, to my unhappiness... lest people reading this think I've been living in la-la land!
>
> If that weren't enough, when we got home after the party that night, my son (who said when I invited him to the party, "Mom, I think a room full of lesbians is more your thing than mine.") had slipped into the house and left a basketful of 70 red roses!

Annalee continues to live in Minnesota.
Interviewer: Arden Eversmeyer

Annalee's son, Steve, and her granddaughter, Shalana, recently celebrated Annalee's 80th birthday by giving her another huge party. They flew in much of her family, and her first love, Marilyn. A few months later, Marilyn and Annalee celebrated 71 years of love and friendship, while Marilyn's daughter held the phone to her ear. "Knowing how she loved to travel, and have new experiences" Annalee said, "I wished her a joyous farewell as we each expressed our last 'I love you' to each other." Marilyn died shortly thereafter.

Mattie Tippit

Born September 1922 in Texas
Interviewed in 2001 at age 78

I haven't missed a damn thing!

I knew I was going to be either a nurse or a doctor when I grew up. I finished high school when I was fifteen, at Tyler High School. I stayed there another year and took a year of postgraduate high school work, simply to get old enough to do what I wanted to do, because I had started school so young. I was not even eighteen yet when I went into nursing school. They let me in early.

Mattie was 21 when she earned her RN, passed the state boards, and began working as the head of a ward in the hospital.

That's where I met the first woman I was ever with. She was a student nurse, and I had just graduated. We had problems. Her mother found out about us, and that was the end of the story.

Even though she had already achieved her goal of becoming a nurse, Mattie went on to enroll at a local university and major in

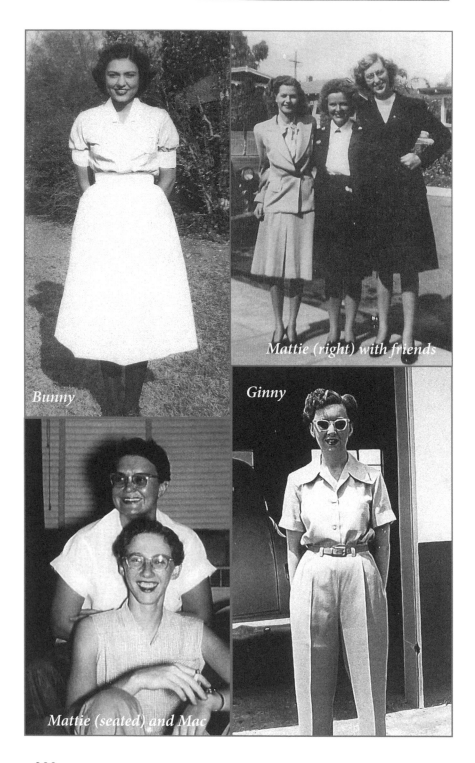

Bunny

Mattie (right) with friends

Ginny

Mattie (seated) and Mac

nursing education. A recent experience with her first lover, Bunny, had left Mattie confused, so once she was back in school, she went to the library in search of answers.

> *Hell, I didn't know anything! So I went to the Sociology Library at the University of Texas, and I found the books I wanted to read. And at the time, for some reason or another, every time I signed my name, I put RN after it, Registered Nurse. And I took these books up, and I said, "I want to check these out." "Well, you can't check these out without an interview with the librarian." And she looked up and said, "Oh, but you're a registered nurse!" and checked them out. … She asked me, "Why do you want them, why this?" I told her I was taking Abnormal Psych.*
>
> *I was at the University of Texas for three semesters. And about that time, they put out the word that they were going to start drafting nurses into the Army. And I said, "Not this child." So I joined the Navy.*
>
> *I read* The Well of Loneliness *when I was in the Navy. Sat up and read all night. Dropped off to sleep about five o'clock, six o'clock in the morning, and was supposed to go on duty in the nurses' quarters at seven. … That was the only book to read. It was the only one. And it had a wrong slant on everything.*
>
> *I finished nursing school in '43, … and in January or February of '45 went into the service and was stationed at the US Naval Hospital in San Diego. My term was for four years. About a year and a half after I had been in, sometime around there, the war was over, World War II was over. And I had signed papers to transfer from the reserves to the regular. But my mother got sick, and I rescinded that request. … So I got out of the Navy early.*

Mattie's sister was now living in California, so instead of returning to Texas, Mattie and a friend stayed with her. It was through that friend that Mattie met Ginny. "I fell head over heels." During her stay in California, Mattie went back to school and began a new career.

I started out as a journalism major and realized, after one semester of it, that was not my bag. So I went into radio and television, and got my degree.... That was when television was in its infancy, so I was in on the ground floor. I didn't make films. I took the films that went on ... and edited them for air presentation.

I really, really enjoyed it. And at that time I was living with Ginny, and it was a good life, it really was a good life.... Ginny and I were together eight and a half years, until I moved back to Texas.

In Texas in 1955, her career path took another sharp turn. She went back to school, this time to the Dallas Institute of Mortuary Science, where she got her Funeral Director and Embalmer licenses, and went to work with her father.

"I did all of my practice, and passed all of my exams for my regular license.... I did some funeral directing, but not much embalming." Her father's funeral home also had an insurance company, and Mattie spent ten years working there. She moved on only after her father retired, and sold the business.

Mickie and Mattie, age 50

Her next job was a year teaching anatomy and health to eighth graders, and then another year teaching language arts to seventh graders. The experience convinced Mattie it was time to go back and finish her master's degree in Education. "I went ahead and finished my master's, and I didn't know what to do. So I just kept going to school, working toward a doctorate." Before she could complete that program however, she stumbled into a position teaching nursing in Lubbock, Texas.

Mattie immediately realized she had found something she loved doing, and stayed in that job for 17 years. She'd also found someone she loved, Mickey. Mattie retired when she was just over 65. Mickey had retired a year or two earlier.

> She had to retire, a medical retirement. She had a heart condition, and they later discovered that she had lymphoma, and then she had breast cancer. The breast cancer went into her lung, the brain, and the bones. She died in 1990. Of course I had retired in '88, and we'd done some things.

Mattie and Mickey traveled as much as they could before Mickey's health wouldn't allow it.

Ginny and Mickey were the two long-term relationships in Mattie's life. There were others, but none that lasted more than a year or two.

> One [relationship] that I would have liked to have had longer was Lisa, but that was too much age difference. There was 49 years difference in our ages [Lisa was the younger], and that doesn't work. You can't take a 23-year-old and put them with the 70s and have it work out. I'd start laughing at something, just haw-hawing, and she'd look at me and say, "What's funny?"
>
> Except for one or two people, my parents met everyone I've ever lived with. I never thought anything less about taking them home. I suppose my parents could have kicked me out, but they weren't built that way. I never came out to them — except for the fact that I took everybody home. But, you know, they're decent people. ... You may be a bitch, or queen, or butch, or whatever in your daily life, but when you're home you're a daughter.

Church always played an important role in Mattie's life, even more so when Mickey was gone. After a series of careers, during which she felt she had to stick with "don't ask, don't tell," it was refreshing to belong to a welcoming church where she could be open and where gay and lesbian people played roles in leadership.

I was sitting downstairs one day [at church], and some woman said, "Well, there are four of us at the table and two of us have never been married." One of them made it very clear that her fiancé was killed in World War II. And the woman said, "Oh, you don't know what you have missed, not being married." And I said, "Yes, I do! I know exactly what I've missed. I haven't missed a damn thing!"

Mattie, at 78, still stays in touch with some of the women in her life, especially Lisa. But she isn't looking for anything new.

I don't have the desire or the energy to do things like that anymore. I don't just sit and twiddle my thumbs—don't misunderstand—but I'm not going to go out and start a new relationship, or anything like that.

I think I've had a really wonderful life. I've done what I wanted to. ... I'm a very fortunate person because of the home life that I had, because of the things I've done in my life, because of the friends I've had in my life.

Mattie Tippit died in 2006.
Interviewer: Arden Eversmeyer

Beverly Todd

Born January 1930 in Michigan
Interviewed in 2001 at age 71

I needed to live a different life than I had been living.

Less than three pounds at birth, Beverly fit comfortably in her unusual bed, a shoebox, with a washcloth for bedding.

> *At that time, hospitals didn't have incubator treatment for preemie babies. They were sent home with the mother, if they survived [childbirth]. ... I survived, so they thought I must have a really strong constitution.*

Beverly and her siblings were raised in a small, autonomous branch of the Baptist church by parents who were "as right-wing as you can find." Her father died when she was just nine, leaving the family destitute.

> *We became a welfare family at that point. And welfare, in those days, consisted almost entirely of commodities: rice, lard, flour. There was a little storefront where people went to get these*

commodities. I felt like we were the only family in our neighbor-hood in this circumstance. My mother was so ashamed that she wouldn't go down and pick up the food, but we children would go with our wagon and get the food, and bring it home. So it was kind of a stigma that I felt. That might not have been there really, but I felt that it was.

When I was maybe eleven or twelve, I began to notice that I wasn't starting to think of boys as my friends were. I was focusing on women and girls as objects of my affection. I knew that this had to be terribly wrong. I was very worried, and my one desire, if I just had enough money, was to go talk to the doctor. He could fix what was broken. ...

By the time I got to high school, away from the little rural school where there were no gyms, and no separate music classes, or art classes, and that kind of thing... I began to find other girls like myself. We never really talked about "it," but we knew about it. Now I had this whole secret world that none of my other friends knew about.... I had the world with ordinary people, and I had this other world with the girls that I discovered in high school, who were not the same as the rest of the world.

Learning she wasn't alone in her feelings helped, but Bev still struggled with negative feelings. "I don't think we knew the word 'lesbian' at that point." It was all so strange to her.

When I got to high school, I started to be involved in sports. I would always play basketball. I played ball with the boys' teams all my grade school life.... Then it was the Second World War, and it was the All American Girls Baseball League. So, of course, I was attracted like a magnet.

Bev got into a training program to help girls improve their baseball skills, and went to a tryout for the big teams. "I really wasn't good enough. I was better than most of the girls in my neighborhood, but not good enough for that professional team." Motivated, Bev just tried harder.

At eighteen, Bev took a vacation from her job at the credit bureau, and met a woman.

We corresponded for a little bit, and I was not judicious in hiding those notes or letters that I got. My mother found them, and called me in. She talked to me and told me that she wished I had never been born, and that she wished she were dead. I think my whole life, from that point on, focused on proving to my mother that I was a normal person.

Bev on the right in 1946

Feeling she had few options, Bev joined the Air Force. Having been raised in a church where she wasn't allowed to cut her hair, go to the movies, play cards, or wear makeup, had prepared her well for the strict Air Force life.

It felt fine to me. ... There were a lot of women there. And being a young woman myself, I probably wasn't as careful as I could have been, but I was pretty careful about my lesbian relationships.

At one point, after about a year and a half or two, I was in a relationship with another woman, and I was transferred from that base. ... We wrote letters and sent them to a third party, who was a civilian, so there would not be that connection for the military to see. We did not carry each other's pictures. We didn't carry each other's addresses. We were extremely careful.

We changed shifts every two days. I did not do well with the changing schedule, and lots of times I had trouble sleeping. I had finished my shift and gone to bed, and my friend was sitting in a chair reading. I heard footsteps coming down the hall and, believe it or not, someone opened the door, and it was the Captain in charge of that unit. She said, "Get up, get dressed and come with me."

They took Chris in one room and took me in another. They told me to sit down in the chair, and the officers of the Office of Special Investigations questioned me for nine hours. ... I knew that they had read my letters and listened to my phone calls, because they could not have known the details otherwise.

I started to cry, and said, "Don't tell my mother," and they just couldn't get me to stop crying. So they took me over to the base hospital and put me down in the basement ward. They came and gave me an injection. I heard voices and when I woke up, I was crying. That went on for about a week.

I heard them talking about transferring me to a civilian mental institution. I remember thinking that if that happens, I will never live through it.

Bev heard of another woman from her barracks that had been taken to a civilian hospital, and two years later she was still there.

If they ever got me into one of those places, I would never get out. ... I just couldn't risk going into any mental institution as a lesbian and have any assurance that I would come out alive. And I just said, "What do you want me to do?" The doctor said, "Well, you have the body of a woman, so we can get you changed around here, and you can see our psychiatrist. If he feels that you can be changed, then we'll talk about it, and I won't toss you out." So I went to the psychiatrist and I told him pretty much what I thought he wanted to hear.

Although Bev managed to stay in the Air Force awhile longer, she was called in for questioning again. "They wanted me to identify the lesbians. I never told them anything about anybody else, but it was just a nightmare."

As part of her mandatory therapy, Bev was told she needed to start going with men, to try to change her life. "There was a man in the weather station where I worked, and he was much more intelligent that most of them. And I was dating him." Bev thought, "This is too painful being a lesbian. I can't do this anymore. ... I really want to change." Marrying the man she'd been dating, Bev quickly became pregnant and received an honorable discharge.

I spent thirty-two years in that marriage, and had five children. I tried to change. I was away from the softball teams [she had played while in the military], and away from all the associations, and I was determined that I was going to be straight, the model citizen. In that marriage, I had five wonderful children.

Working as a meter maid 1969

Once her children were in school all day, in addition to being a homemaker and working full time outside the home, Bev went back to college herself. She didn't do it to get a better job, but to study something she loved. Bev majored and minored in English, and it took her about ten years to graduate.

At a local independent bookstore, Bev found her calling, working with books.

I started my book group, and I began to know some people who were lesbians. I was in a real turmoil. By then my children were grown and on their own. I had just such intense feelings, I didn't know what to do, and my husband knew that something was different.

He was terribly upset. It was terrible, and we separated. Now I was out on my own. It was like a second coming out for me. ... I needed to live as who I was for the rest of the time I have.

She moved out and began living alone. Bev also began working at the public library. Leading an independent life also meant she had to explain things to her children.

I told them a little bit about the circumstances, and that I had remained a lesbian all those years. And this was a time when I needed to live a different life than I had been. I felt like the children were all very gracious. No one dropped me out of their life, or anything like that. But it was a difficult time.

Bev's life changed dramatically when one of her daughters was diagnosed with cancer. With the support of friends, she was able to take her daughter back to her remote cabin in Alaska where she died, surrounded by seed catalogs, and making plans for where the tulips should be planted. The weeks she spent in Alaska with her daughter were incredibly taxing, and at the same time fulfilling.

About a year and a half after I came out, I met another librarian. She was considerably younger than I am. . . . I didn't see other women out there my age. I went to meetings and potlucks in Boulder, but there were very few women in my age group that I could form a relationship with. So I had a three-year relationship with this librarian. It was great. But our ages made a difference to me, and it made a difference to her. I knew this wasn't going to be a lifetime love.

She [the librarian] introduced me to Tobi. That was a life-changing experience, let me tell you. That has been the biggest joy. I have never ever met a person like her. She makes me laugh. . . . We had a great time courting, and we were together for a year and we decided on a commitment ceremony.

Tobi had been a city girl, but quickly took to a more low-key existence in Estes Park with Bev. "It's just been a blossoming I feel in my life, to have her in my life."

Tobi had come into the relationship with some serious physical challenges, and she and Bev talked several times about who would die first, and who would handle it better. Together, they developed a large circle of friends. Bev's children saw how happy Tobi made her and loved her for it . . . until there was "a strange turn of events."

Bev suddenly became seriously ill. It took four days for the hospital to discover a perforated bowel, and by then peritonitis had developed. Doctors were not sure Bev would survive the surgery.

> *I guess [the children] were scared and didn't know what to do, and wanted to be the ones who made the decisions. Tobi was scared, but she had the power of attorney, and she was making decisions. Then, instead of being like* Little House on the Prairie, *where the family pulled together when someone was in trouble, there was a definite wedge pushing everyone in different directions. It was extremely hard on me when Tobi started to tell me about it. I had not known that all this was going on. I just said, "I feel like I'm being pulled apart here."*

After the crisis was over, Tobi wanted Bev to write to her children making Tobi's role in her life clear. "It's not always family closing around you. Sometimes it is the family pulling in different directions. Tobi's only comment was, 'If I were a husband, I don't

Courting Tobi (on the right) in 1989

think the rift would have happened.'" Bev didn't think that had anything to do with it, but knew "as generous as they are, as loving as they are, they are a part of this culture."

Bev acquiesced, telling her children that if she were ever in a similar situation, Tobi was to make the decisions Bev couldn't make for herself. After some initial strain, everyone returned to being friends.

> *I didn't want to have to make a decision between the children and Tobi. ... The children have a place in my life, and Tobi has a place. And those are two different places. There is not one that is more important, ... I want them all in my life.*

One of the many things Tobi brought into Bev's life was an increased interest in activism. "I'm certainly not the activist Tobi is, but I am active. ... We are more aware of places where we need to be active. Let people know what we want, and what we call valuable."

Bev was involved in trying to get the local school board to add sexual orientation to their non-discrimination policy. After carefully pointing out that "we're people that need to have the same rights as others," Bev was dismayed to hear the board member reply, "It is not right. It is okay to be black, but it is not okay to be gay or lesbian." But she hasn't given up, and introduces the issue each year. "It may take a long time."

Music, especially singing, was always a part of Bev's life. From early childhood, and throughout her married life, Bev always found time to sing in a local choir. A highlight in her life was traveling to San Jose to participate in a huge festival of choirs. "That was just one of the very most wonderful times of my life." Another constant through the thirty-plus years she has lived in Estes Park, is Bev's love of hiking in nearby Rocky Mountain National Park, and she and Tobi had their commitment ceremony there.

"My life is very full. I love being seventy, because I was not sure I was going to get there."

One of the gifts at her 70th birthday party was what Bev describes as "a silly, little blow-up doll."

We deflated it after the party and put it in a box. I was taking some boxes to a local UPS mailing place to recycle, and later they called us and said, "I think we have something here that you didn't intend to recycle." It was the doll. We had made a mistake and just left that in the box. The clerk said, "Stop by and ask for Betty Blow-me." I went to the shop, and she had this wicked smile on her face!

Life is good. I'm enjoying it, and sometimes I say, "Wow!" There were a lot of years when I wasn't enjoying it, but I had five children, one who has died. And I don't have any complaints. Life has been full. Lots of sad times. Lots of totally wonderful times. And I'm glad I'm here.... This is part of the best time. It has been a truly fulfilling time. I think I've helped some people along the way. I hope that I have.

Beverly continues to live in Colorado. Tobi Hale died in 2005. Interviewer: Arden Eversmeyer

.

Irene
Weiss

**Born August 1926
in Pennsylvania
Interviewed in 2001 at age 77**

You, with the gray hair!

---

*My family had a book written by one of the early psycho-
analysts, Wilhelm Stekel. Don't ask me what my family was
doing with that book. I have no idea. It was about four inches
thick. I was about twelve when I read it. Now, I didn't understand everything I read, but I understood enough to know
that he was describing me when he talked about 'inverts'. It
just came to me in a flash that that was what my feelings were
about, and that's who I was. So at a very early age, I thought of
myself as a homosexual. And I had little crushes on girls forever
after that.*

Irene tried dating boys, but it was a struggle. "It was a rank
failure. I was bored with them. Totally bored!" So at 15 years of
age, she accepted who she was. "It might be bad, but that is who I
am.... From then on, I knew I was a lesbian."

Although Irene had already admitted to herself she was a lesbian, she tried not to act on it. Irene wanted to enter nurse training after graduating from high school, but was afraid living with all those women would be too much of a test of her resolve. "I knew, I was positive, that I wanted to be alone with women in a room at night." A family friend convinced her to enter a nursing program, and her fears came true.

"I wasn't even there a week before I was having a sexual relationship with one of the other girls, who was a little more experienced than I was. She pushed me right over that edge."

Nurse training tested Irene academically, and she found herself loving it, staying near the top of her class. But nursing school also brought a number of relationships with women, and a big crush on a female teacher.

She knew it and tried to explain to me how it was wrong, blah, blah, blah. By that time I was no longer feeling that it was bad to be a lesbian. One girl got kicked out because of our relationship, and I was saved because I was younger, and they assumed I was led into it, which was totally wrong! And then in my senior year, I fell in love with a patient of mine. I seduced her, I guess. She was a married woman with two children.

After carrying on the affair for quite a while, Irene got a frantic phone call from the woman in the middle of the night. She had confessed the affair to her husband, who had promptly thrown her out clothed only in her nightgown. Irene sneaked her into the nurse's residence to stay with her. Weeks later, the woman's family essentially kidnapped her, and told the administration about the situation. Luckily, the school allowed Irene to resign.

I went home and told my family. I told them that I was in love with Phyllis, and that I loved her like a man loves a woman. I didn't know how else to say it. My mother was shocked. My father was stunned. ... This was 1948-49.

My father said, "How could you not control your animal appetites?" ... Then he said I should have drowned myself before I came home and told him that.

Telling her family she had applied for a job in New York, Irene was encouraged to go ahead and leave home, since she had disgraced them. Then her mother relented, and tried to talk her into staying, essentially hiding out, but Irene had other plans.

Irene got the job in New York, quickly identified a fellow lesbian, and was introduced to the Village. There she met, and became involved with, another married woman — this time, one who was trying to escape her marriage. Living together in various parts of New York City, Irene and her friend noticed lesbians who didn't seem to be working.

> We kind of watched them, and we saw they would cater to the tourists, and the tourists would buy them drinks, and things like that. We thought we could do that, so we both quit our jobs. Naive and stupid! We found out what the girls did for a living, which was hooking. … It shocked us both. That shows how young we still were.

When they grew tired of subsisting on tamale pies and corn flakes, Irene and her friend decided to take what little money they had left and leave for somewhere warm and sunny. They headed toward California, but the girls' funds took them only as far as Iowa, where they got jobs for the winter. They scraped together enough money to buy a 1936 Buick, and, after delaying long enough for Irene to get a driver's permit (neither of them had known how to drive), they made their way to California.

Irene worked at a variety of nursing positions over the next decade or two, never

In her butch finery in 1952

• 225 •

Working as a nursing administrator in 1971

Irene, on the right, at 45

quite happy with the jobs or the schedule. Finally, she found a job with regular hours. "It was in a nursing home. I didn't even know what a nursing home was, but I went to work there because I could work Monday through Friday on the day shift. I learned a lot." Finding her niche, Irene learned the business side as well as the practice of nursing, and took on the accounting for the facility.

In the meantime, I had several relationships. I never had any relationship that lasted longer than five years. … That was okay for me. I ended up thinking that's who I am, and that's okay.

The nursing home where Irene worked expanded, and as it did, she took advantage of the opportunity to learn budgeting, staffing, reading construction plans, and more, becoming a valuable asset to the company. The owner promised her part ownership of the next expansion, in return for all her extra work. He was true to his word and, for a relatively small amount, Irene made what turned out to be an incredibly successful investment. Income from this investment allowed Irene more time to devote to improving the lives of others. She was very active in the California Nursing Organization.

I was very instrumental in legitimizing nursing home nurses, because they were looked down upon by other nurses. I worked with the Public Health Department and Social Services Department to raise standards of care, and ensure standards were enforced.

I found out that I could move people, and that I could influence people's thinking.

Enjoying this creative period of her career, Irene made lots of new friends, many of them lesbians. Feminism was just beginning to thrive when Irene and her much-younger girlfriend braved the crowds to hear Kate Millet read from one of her books.

> *The place was jammed. We had to stand. During the break, someone was gesturing to me from across the room, and I didn't know it. I thought she was talking to someone else. And I turned around and looked, and she said, "No, you, with the gray hair!" And I thought, "Who is this talking to me about my gray hair?"... "You, with the gray hair," she says, "I want you to come to my older women's group." I said, "Older woman?" No one had ever called me that. I was stunned. And she got to me finally, and stuck a flyer in my hand. And it was Marilyn Murphy, of course. Bold and brassy as she always was.*

Irene went, not because it was for older women, but because of Marilyn. "I did go to her group, but only to flirt with her." Since both Irene and Marilyn were already with other women, they just became good friends. Marilyn introduced her to the women's movement, acting as her mentor, taking her along to various functions. When they were both single again, Irene and Marilyn began what they later jokingly called "a brief affair which lasted decades."

Irene had learned, through her earlier activist work with nursing, that she was a good writer and speaker. Together, she and Marilyn embarked on a remarkable journey, devoting themselves to the women's movement. They were an essential part of the Califia Community, a radical feminist educational collective, known for its week-long retreats.

> *I learned to relate to other women as a woman. I had always kept myself separate from other women. I was a lesbian, not a woman with a husband and children in a conventional lifestyle. I had never thought of myself as being like other women in any way, but I was. ... I learned that at Califia, and I learned that from Marilyn. ... For most women, it was a life changing experience. It certainly was for me.*

What we did was hold three-day-long sessions for women to learn about the women's movement. The purpose was to address the issues that divided women, and we saw those as racism, classism and sexism. That's what the purpose of it was, to discuss some of those things, and to break down some of the barriers, so that women could begin to work together for the benefit of all women. Get past the things that kept us apart. That was the greatest learning experience of my life.

They continued this work for five or six years, learning as much as they were teaching. At the same time that Irene and Marilyn were involved in Califia, they formed Southern California Women for Understanding, and held programs at their home; out of that came other important programs such as a rape crisis center. "It originated in our garage, which we had converted into a meeting room. All sorts of things emerged there, like Women Against Racism, a group that still functions."

With Marilyn in 1986

As exciting as all this was, Irene and Marilyn found themselves exhausted, and in need of a break, so when a friend offered the use of a small motor home for a week, they took her up on it.

We borrowed it, and we went away for a few days, and we fell in love with that idea. Five months later, we bought our own little motor home. It was a tiny little motor home, only seventeen feet long, and that was the size with the engine and everything! ... It had an over-the-cab bed, and it had a toilet, and it had a sink, and a refrigerator and a chair to sit in. ... We loved it!

A year-long adventure brought them a new understanding of the outdoors. Irene and Marilyn had been seriously bitten by the travel bug, and were ready to let others take over the work at Califia. They embarked on a three-year odyssey, exploring the country and women's communities. Then, feeling a need to settle for a while, they bought a bungalow at Pagoda By the Sea, in Florida. "Pagoda was a community of all women, and this was a radical separatist community; no men allowed there."

Irene and Marilyn were surprised to realize they had to struggle to find their place in the community, and to make friends.

It took a long time for the women there to accept us, which was distressing because we thought we were such big shots back home. We didn't realize that, at our age, it would be harder to make friends. But we did eventually, and ended up liking living there.

There was much about living collectively that was difficult. I don't think any of us has perfected that yet, and probably never will. People come with different expectations. We may all be lesbians, but boy we're sure different!

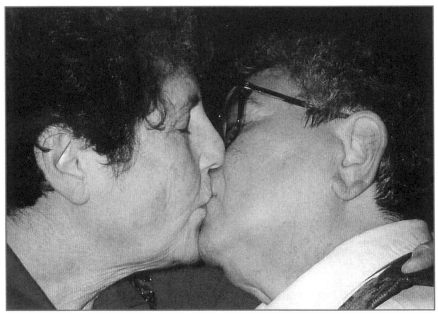

Marilyn and Irene, 1990

Pagoda had been started by women who wanted a place to do theater, and the main house was converted for performances downstairs, and living quarters upstairs. During their seven year stay, Irene and Marilyn were the driving force behind raising funds to remodel Pagoda, improving accessibility at the same time.

The next phase of their big adventure came in the early 1990s, when they moved from Florida, and spent much of their time promoting sales of a book. "It was a collection of her [Marilyn's] essays from the *Lesbian News* in Southern California. I played her tour promoter for awhile. I contacted all the women's bookstores in the United States and sent them information about Marilyn." Offering to visit and do book readings, the two of them set off on two tours of the country.

As they were traveling for the book tour, Irene and Marilyn visited friends living in another women's community in Arizona. Like their friends, they fell in love with the place, and moved. "We moved to Superstition Mountain Resort. It was right across the street from The Pueblo.... When we came to visit, there were sixty women on the waiting list for The Pueblo." Even though it was an all-woman community, the transition wasn't easy.

> *It was a big culture shock for me, coming from a radical separatist community, and our experiences at Califia were also pretty radical. To come to a place where most of the lesbians were not radical, and some of them couldn't even call them-selves lesbians.... I was shocked.*

Irene tried to talk Marilyn into leaving. Instead, Marilyn convinced Irene they needed to stay, and make it better, and some things did improve. Irene knows there are trade-offs, but she still misses that radical slice of her past life.

Soon after they had settled in Arizona, Irene began to notice Marilyn was having some vision and cognitive issues. Marilyn had always been a bright, articulate, outgoing woman and something just wasn't right. Even though several doctors didn't find anything serious, they continued to seek an explanation. Finally, it was determined that Marilyn had had a small stroke, and her abilities slowly degenerated over the next five years.

I've become her caretaker now. The worst part of it is her brain is not gone; her thinking processes are not gone. It's the other stuff that is gone. And she knows what she's lost. . . . She was a woman who lived in her head, she was a thinker, a writer, a philosopher, a political person, gregarious, a teacher, all of that. And it's all gone. And she knows it.

I don't know how she does it. I'm hard of hearing, and I wear a hearing aid. She speaks very low sometimes . . . and I can't get it. It's very difficult for both of us.

Even though the last few years were especially difficult, Irene sums up their twenty-seven years together saying, "Marilyn was everything I ever wanted."

Irene continues to live in Arizona. Marilyn died in 2004.
Interviewer: Arden Eversmeyer

Addenda

The Story Behind the Project

Arden Eversmeyer is the heart and soul of the Old Lesbian Oral Herstory Project. It's not surprising that this impressive enterprise was an outgrowth of her personal experiences, and passions. In preparing for this book, I was granted the opportunity to sit with Arden and give her a taste of her own medicine. In essence, I was able to interview the interviewer!

With tape recorder running, Arden shared the story behind the Project. The best way to understand the Project, and how it developed, is to read Arden's own words. What follows is the majority of the transcript of that November 2008 interview.

Text from the full interview, as well as an audio sample, will be posted at the Old Lesbian Oral Herstory Project website: www.olohp.org/aboutarden.html

M = Margaret Purcell, and A = Arden Eversmeyer
(In some cases, names have been changed to initials or first names only.)

M: Tell me how the project was born.

A: The project was born because, here in the Houston women's social group of LOAF, Lesbians Over Age Fifty, we suddenly had two or three women with very serious health problems. One of our members said, "Arden. Why don't we get all of these women to write a mini-autobiography of themselves?" We tried to do that, and it didn't work… nobody ever has anything to say about their own lives.

In the meantime, one of the women did, indeed, die. I still regret not having gotten her life story. Then in 1996, OLOC [Old Lesbians Organizing for Change] had its first Gathering. Attending was Degania Golove, from the Los Angeles area. She was connected with the June Mazer Lesbian Archives. I shared with her my efforts to get mini-bios, and that we still had a couple of women I was sorely concerned about, and that I would love to have their stories. She got real excited about it, and she told me she'd send me some materials. Ultimately, I also got some more information on oral history work off the Internet.

M: That was in 1996?

A: '96, yes. My first oral history interview was in 1998 with Marie Mariano here in Houston. That was a learning experience!

Since then, there has been a refining of the way I work. There's been a change in the kind of questions I ask. Marie was wide open and receptive, so it was not a problem. But that is not always the case with some of these women.

M: I thought that what motivated you was that you had given your own interview.

A: No. I even forgot about that. I was well into the [history] project, and somebody said, "Well, Arden. Have you been interviewed?" I said, "No," but then I remembered that I had agreed to do an interview with a friend, a mature student at the University of Houston who was in the Women's Studies Program. Her assignment was to do an oral history. The professor had told them, "Now, these people need to have a history" and that "they certainly don't if they're 21!"

That happened in 1990. We did the interview, she gave me a copy of the paper that she turned in, and I stuck it in a filing cabinet and forgot about it. Later, that 1990 interview was the basis for the first part of what became my book in the collection. Then in the late 90s, her partner interviewed me for an addendum to what had happened since 1990. And, of course, that became outdated after I began the Oral Herstory Project.

M: What motivated the second interviewer? Was she a student?

A: No. She just wanted to do it. She did one of the other interviews that's in the collection, [Helen Cathcart], as part of her doctoral dissertation.

M: Is there a recording of either of your own interviews?

A: No.

M: That's too bad. When did this become known as the Herstory Project? And why "herstory" instead of "history"?

A: It got its name when the OLOC Steering Committee approached me in 2000 about adopting my work as a major project for the organization. I was doing it on my own, and they said they could subsidize part of the expenses for me. We called it the Old Lesbian Oral Herstory Project, adopting the word "herstory" as a feminist statement. History has written out women so much.

M: Did you always have the same criteria as to who was going to be interviewed?

A: That's gotten a little more refined. I used the OLOC database as a starting place for finding more old lesbians.

M: Are there certain pieces of information you want to get from each interview?

A: I was looking at discovering information on how women were finding each other. We all agreed that there certainly wasn't any information network out there. We didn't have periodicals and organizations like we have today. So that began to form the information I was looking for, and focused my efforts on women who were born before 1930.

M: Was 70 years of age your cutoff? Or born before 1930?

A: Seventy became the magic number. Today, in 2008, we laugh when a woman reaches her 70th birthday and was born in 1938! Time moves so quickly.

     I have interviewed women who were younger, whose stories I felt were really important to have in the collection. For instance, a woman who had been put in a mental hospital and given "the cure." There are quite a few women who have experienced that and not many who will talk about it. Those experiences are an important part of our lesbian history.

M: Have you always had a goal, or a sense of what you want to come from the Project? Or has that evolved?

A: It just happened as this thing grew, and as we started getting more and more of these completed stories. Somebody said, "Why don't you write a book?" The idea to write a book just took on a life of its own. It was nothing that I ever envisioned, let alone a website, for goodness sake!

M: How do you think the women who gave their stories feel about their involvement?

A: Almost without exception, when they get their book [a copy of the completed Herstory] back, they're pleased. I get the nicest letters and e-mails. They are happy with the end product, and the time and energy that they have contributed to it. There's only been one, out of all these women, who, when she saw her book, was surprised at what she had done with her life.

Jennie always said she'd never done anything, and she'd wished she hadn't done the story. And that's Jennie. She really never acknowledged that she came from a working class background; she had to leave town, her home, to have a life; she worked her way through school; she became a school teacher; she bought her own home in San Francisco, for goodness sake; she was an activist, involved in the AIDS thing. But she has never seen her life as something positive.

M: She has a fantastic story. I was so taken with her.

A: That is the only one who said she was sorry she did it.

M: Even so, she gave you full permission?

A: Oh, yeah.

M: How did you come up with your set of questions? And have they changed over time?

A: They have changed to some extent. I originally had some questions that were very personal, and I got a sense of women backing away. At first, I would always ask somebody if she saw herself as a gay woman or a lesbian, or neither. I had a question about identifying as butch or femme. Well, you don't ask that. Sometimes, just talking about their lives, there is no question where they would fall on the scale. So I took that out pretty quickly.

M: I've noticed in reading the transcripts, that you very seldom ask anything about them being lesbian until they bring it up. And even then, you really don't try to draw that out specifically.

A: Because it's not about sex.

M: Or even about sexuality?

A: Right. They *are* being interviewed because they are lesbian. That's an upfront criteria. But to talk about sexuality in any way that would seem like talking about sex, … I have found I learned more by not being specific, than if I asked a question and the woman backed away.

It has to do with having a little bit of time to sit and visit before we ever start. I would say that in 75% of the interviews that I've done, I hadn't met the woman before interview time. So she needs to know something about me. I tell her anything she wants to know. That way she's a little more relaxed. It gives her more of a feeling of security to know something about me, and about the Project, and that I'm not going to go home and say, "Let me tell you about who I met…" You know? It pays dividends to spend time with the woman before the interview.

M: Are the interviews usually done in their homes?

A: Usually. A woman in Florida came to the motor home we often travel in on our story-gathering trips. She had an adult son living in her home who "did not approve" of her. But for the most part, I go to the woman's home. And it helps. I want her sitting in her favorite chair, relaxed.

M: Do you think that the questions you ask are shaped by your own life experiences?

A: Of course. We come from the generation and era where concepts like "butch/femme" were important. We all came out of that era, and I understand it. Someone younger than me, talking to them, would not have had that experience, and would not understand why we are who we are.

M: I would think there is a value to being an old lesbian asking questions and conducting the interview.

A: You have to have some common life experiences with these women to know what to ask them; otherwise, they're going to tell you things that you don't begin to understand. I think it makes a big difference. I think I get more information because of my age.

M: I know you've had interviews [contributed to the Project] from a couple of other interviewers. Do you see much difference in their interviewing style?

A: They're going to have their own style, but they're using my outline. If I train an interviewer, she has the outline of the information I want to get in the interview. With every interview, a question can lead off in different directions. As long as we get that track of growing up, and how we began, anything extraneous that the interviewer can bring in as a result of one of those questions is good.

M: I think the women who have volunteered to share their stories are doing an exceptional service to the community.

A: I do, too. It's one thing to be comfortable, and live with who you are with some discretion, not revealing yourself unnecessarily, and it's quite another to say, "This is who I am," and then to see it in print. I have friends here, life-long lesbians, who will not do an interview. I find them to be the most homophobic of the group. The women who came out later have struggled with identity and sexuality. They're more in tune with saying, "This is who I am."

M: But you're not talking about them being homophobic toward other people, are you?

A: Just themselves. In saying, "This is who I am." And there are lots of reasons for this to happen. Much of it's due to religion, of course. Dealing with the guilt and shame heaped upon us. And some of it's cultural. Some of these women … Heavens! They played softball, you know!

M: I know there's an introduction letter and outline sent beforehand to the woman giving an interview.

A: After the initial arrangements are made, I mail her a copy of the outline that I use in the interviews. I send it to her, and I tell her, "I don't want you to write anything." That happened once, and it got read to me! I suggest she use the outline to collect memories and make notes. I also encourage her to gather any documentation.

M: How much guidance do you give them about documentation?

A: I tell them that I would love pictures, and any kind of certificates or awards. Really, anything, starting with their birth and going through their life to current time. I tell them that there is no such thing as too many pictures. They provide a feel of how the woman grew up, what she looked like, and what was going on.

M: Are there usually places nearby where you can take the documentation and get it copied?

A: If time allows, I like to take the documents, copy them, and leave them with the owner. Otherwise, I bring them home with me, and do the copy work here. The woman identifies the pictures and things for me before I leave. I try to get them back within two days. I do not want that stuff lying around.

Finding transcribers is a problem. I've had heterosexual women, I've had lesbians, I've had two males. Somebody thinks they want to do it, but it turns out to be more than they thought it was going to be. I don't type, so it's a no brainer for me.

M: The interviewees, the women that you talk with, have they ever expressed any concern about who is transcribing?

A: No. I tell them it's transcribed from audio tape or digital recording to the written text, and that they'll get a copy of the first draft. Then it's up to them to edit. I say, "Now don't be distressed. We all have speech idioms." And almost all of them say, "I didn't know I talk like that!"

M: I know you've mentioned that you can't justify traveling for just one interview. Is cost ever a deciding factor on doing an interview?

Working on reassembling Herstories after they were taken apart to create a digital backup. Left to right: Arden Eversmeyer, Janice L. Ives (Scottie's Janice), and Ellen Goodrich.

A: Not at this point. I have made a practice, if Charlotte and I are going to an event, we try to have a couple of interviews either en route or there. We've had interviews every time we've gone to the National Women's Music Festival. That really works.

M: You've said that an interview or two got messed up. Was it a recorder problem?

A: It was an attached mic that had a short in the wires. And I got home with blank tapes. That hurt my feelings!

M: The few that this has happened to ... have they been more than willing to talk to you again?

A: Oh, yes.

M: Do you feel their story has changed?

A: Basically, they were the same, but they were more relaxed. It's paid dividends. The redos get costly, in terms of having to do the travel, but it's paid dividends, led to more interviews.

M: Where in the [interview] process is the contract signed?

A: First up. When we're visiting, when I first get there. I say, "We need a contract with you. And you, on faith, are going to have to believe that I will honor that." I tell her that there are two kinds of contracts. I get one of each out, and I put them in front of her so she can read them. Before I leave there, I want one of those contracts back.

M: I noticed you have a couple of interview contracts that say their stories can't be used for anything.

A: There is one.

M: Do you have any regrets that you spent the time and money to get a story that the woman doesn't ever want you to use?

A: No.

M: I'm sure at some point the stories will be permanently archived. How will it work when there is a story in the collection with a conditional contract?

A:	I think at such time as these books are moved to a permanent home, we'll have to flag books. They can't be used for research, but they are part of the collection. Finding an appropriate archive is a whole project in itself.

M:	Has the subject of using pseudonyms been a discussion with many women?

A:	Only once or twice. I would dearly love to have one friend's story. I've talked to her over the years, and she is just locked down. She thinks nobody in her little city knows about her. I have told her that we could do it anonymously, with no name and no pictures and she just can't. I would do it anonymously if she'd let me.

M:	Have women expressed concerns about outing someone else in the process of telling their story?

A:	That is part of the beauty of the woman getting the first draft. I say to her when we're doing this, "You do not need to be careful about your pronouns and things, because you have the ability to take out of the interview, once it is in draft form, anything you don't want in there." So that covers outing and any "oops," you know. I tell them all that up front, so they're not constantly sitting there worrying about what they say.

M:	Have you noticed this kind of editing happening?

A:	Oh, yeah. The woman just didn't feel comfortable with using a name, because she didn't have that person's permission, or whatever. So we took it out.

M:	Has anyone ever changed her mind, once you started the process?

A:	Yes. We had an appointment with a woman, an ex-college professor. She was so sweet. We actually parked the motor home in her driveway, spent the night, and had a wonderful dinner with her. She just got cold feet. That's okay. That was just where she was at that time. She felt bad about changing her mind, since we had driven there. It happens.

M: There is one story you call your "half-interview." Do you feel the woman changed her mind, and that's why there was so little information?

A: No. She didn't know how to talk. And there wasn't any kind of a lead-in question, that I tried, that would get her to start talking.

M: About the terms "gay," "lesbian," "queer," … do you have to feel people out to see what words they want used?

A: Oh yeah. In some ways, that tells me where they are, and how they feel about themselves. And, to some extent, if there is internalized homophobia, that we may have to work around that during the interview. For the most part, unless they were living in urban areas where there was gay activism going on, San Francisco or New York, most of these women were "gay women." They weren't "lesbians."

M: You talked about how it was such a learning experience to do your first interview. Are you totally comfortable now when you do interviews?

A: Oh, yes. I look forward to it. I love meeting them.

M: Have you learned tricks as to how to deal with people who don't really want to talk much about themselves, how to draw information out of them?

A: If I feel a resistance to talking about something, I tend not to pursue it. I don't want to risk a woman's comfort level, or get to where she doesn't want to finish the interview.

M: Does anyone seem bothered by the tape recorder sitting there?

A: I had one who talked to the recorder for awhile, and then she finally quit, finally forgot about it.

M: Is it hard not to interject your own comments?

A: Not anymore. During the first two or three interviews, when I saw them in written form, I thought, "Well, who the hell's interview is this?" With Marie, she's saying something, and I'd say, "Oh, yes." Then I'd give my parallel experience. Adding your own experiences is easy to do, unless you stay aware. Instead, I make notes of something we need to talk about later. Then, when we have a little break, or we finish, I say, "You said something about ...." But oh yes. I did a lot of talking at first.

M: Do you find it harder to interview a woman you know personally?

A: I don't think so.

M: How long does an interview usually take?

A: It varies. Sometimes an hour and a half, sometimes half a day.

M: Do you sit straight through interviews, or take breaks?

A: Up front, I tell them, "If we need to take a break, all you have

Arden speaking about the project in 2006; Ocie Perry, in the foreground, holding a small display board based on her own story.

to do is say it's time." Most of the taping usually can be done in a couple of hours. And there's an understanding, that if anything needs to be added we can do it.

M: I wanted to ask a little more about the transcription. How do you find people to be transcribers?

A: Miracles.

M: Did you start out with people you knew?

A: Well, I contacted a lesbian who taught at the University of Houston in the Women's Studies program, and told her I needed transcribers. Out of that, I got the wife of one of the professors, and she did two or three, and that was just too much. Another woman transcribed for me for a long time. Then a friend connected me with a woman in Santa Cruz, California. She has been working for me for a couple of years. She does good work, and she's fast. Waiting to get an interview transcribed makes me crazy. I want things to move.

M: Once you've done your part, you want somebody else to do their part!

A: I want it to keep moving. And then, of course, there is that unknown thing that happens, once you send a transcript back to be edited. You may never see it again. There are a few of those.

This was the end of the recording, but not the end of our conversations. We are in constant contact through e-mail, and I learn more about Arden, and the Old Lesbian Herstory Project, almost every day.

More and more stories will be gathered, and added to the collection, as long as Arden is willing and able. She has trained several other women to do interviews, and hopes the project will continue, even when she's no longer involved. But if it doesn't, she's okay with that. She's comfortable with what she has accomplished, and proud that there will be at least some record of the unique lives these women have led.

With luck, this history is far from over. Just as those women have gone on to have a variety of new experiences, so does the Oral Herstory Project. The Project has a life of its own, and hopefully, will continue to grow for years to come.

The OLOHP Website: www.olohp.org

Sharing the stories in the Old Lesbian Oral Herstory Project has always been one of its main goals. To that end, with the help of friends and supporters, the Project now has its own website. The site, found at www.olohp.org, has a wide array of information about the OLOHP including brief profiles and photos from some of the Herstories. As time allows, more profiles will be added as well as audio clips.

The OLOHP Books

A Gift of Age: Old Lesbian Life Stories is the first of three books that are currently in development. Each book will feature 20 to 25 stories based on the interviews.

Whereas *A Gift of Age* presents a representative cross-section from the various interviews in the collection, additional work will focus on interviews with couples, both of whom have given interviews for this project. After that, we plan to share stories of "early and late bloomers" — women who came out very early in their lives, and women who came out in their 50s, 60s or even later.

Send us your e-mail, or mailing address, and we'll be glad to let you know as each book becomes available.

OLOHP
PO Box 980422
Houston, TX 77098
e-mail info@olohp.org
www.olohp.org

OLOC and the OLOHP

OLOC, Old Lesbians Organizing for Change, is mentioned quite a few times in this book, for several reasons. OLOC is unique in its dedication to improving the lives of old lesbians for the past twenty years. For much of that time, it was the only organization devoted to old lesbians, so it isn't surprising that many of the women interviewed for the Old Lesbian Oral Herstory Project were a part of OLOC.

Arden served on the OLOC Steering Committee for 14 years, many of those years as a Co-Director. Although she had developed this project independently, OLOC was aware of her work. It was at an OLOC event that Arden first sought advice on structuring the project, from a woman who worked at a lesbian archive. As the project developed, Arden would occasionally submit excerpts from Herstories to the OLOC newsletter.

OLOC saw the importance of Arden's project, and in 2002, entered into a role of sponsorship of the OLOHP. In addition to giving financial support, OLOC was able to assist Arden in identifying women who might be willing to share their stories.

The relationship between the two, OLOC and OLOHP, has been greatly beneficial to both. When Arden is no longer able to continue with the Old Lesbian Oral Herstory Project, ownership will be transferred to OLOC.

Here is the contact information for anyone interested in learning more about Old Lesbians Organizing for Change:

OLOC
PO Box 5853
Athens, OH 45701
info@oloc.org
www.oloc.org

Cross Reference

In lieu of a traditional index, we opted to provide our own version—more of a cross reference rather than an index. We hope it's helpful.

Stories by Women's Year of Birth

1916 Helen Cathcart
1918 Betty Shoemaker
1919 Ruth Silver
1919 Beverly Hickok
1921 Skip Neal
1922 Marie Mariano
1922 Mattie Tippit
1923 Vera Martin
1924 Ricci Bronson
1924 Betty Rudnick
1925 Jean Mountaingrove
1926 Ocie Perry
1926 Irene Weiss
1927 Jenny Gates
1927 Annalee Stewart
1928 LeClair Bissell
1928 Tre Ford
1930 Beverly Todd
1934 Charlotte Doclar
1934 Scottie Scott
1936 Lois Heindselman
1936 Sally Duplaix

If you are an old lesbian who would like more information on sharing your story with the Old Lesbian Oral Herstory Project, or if you know someone who might be interested, here is our contact information:

 OLOHP
PO Box 980422
Houston, TX 77098
e-mail info@olohp.org
www.olohp.org

Order Form

Three Easy Ways to Order:

- Order online at www.olohp.org
- Download an order form at www.olohp.org
- Mail this order form with payment information to OLOHP

Make checks payable to OLOHP	Shipping
OLOHP **PO Box 980422** **Houston, TX 77098**	Inside US: $4 for 1 book $2 each additional book Out of US: varies, ask *Usually ships in 48-72 hours*

Bill To (as it appears on check or credit card)

Name:

Address:

City: State: Zip:

Phone:

E-mail:

Ship To (if different than above)

Name:

Address:

City: State: Zip:

☐ Check   ☐ Money Order   ☐ MasterCard   ☐ Visa

Credit Card Number	Expiration Date
☐☐☐☐ ☐☐☐☐ ☐☐☐☐ ☐☐☐☐	☐☐ ☐☐

Item	Unit Cost	Quantity	Total
A Gift of Age ISBN 978-0-9823669-6-7	$16.95 (US dollars)		
	Sales Tax (TX residents add 8.25%)		
	Shipping & Handling (see rates listed above)		
		Order Total	

Discount available for bulk orders.

The Old Lesbian Oral Herstory Project • www.olohp.org
 PO Box 980422 • Houston, TX 77098 • info@olohp.org

mail in an order or share this form with a friend